Chasen's

Chasen's

WHERE HOLLYWOOD DINED
RECIPES & MEMORIES

BETTY GOODWIN
DESIGN BY SHERYL WINTER

ANGEL CITY PRESS

ANGEL CITY PRESS, INC.

Published by Angel City Press
2118 Wilshire Boulevard, Suite 880
Santa Monica, California 90403
310-395-9982

FIRST PUBLISHED IN 1996 BY ANGEL CITY PRESS

1 3 5 7 9 10 8 6 4 2

FIRST EDITION

ISBN 1-883318-23-8

Art direction and design: Sheryl Winter

LIBRARY OF CONGRESS CATALOGING-IN-PUBLICATION DATA

Goodwin, Betty.
   Chasen's, where Hollywood dined : recipes and memories / by Betty
Goodwin. 1st ed.
      p.   cm.
   Includes indexes.
   ISBN 1883318238
   1. Chasen's (Restaurant)--California--Los Angeles--History.
2. Cookery.   I. Title.
TX945.5.C37G66 1996
641.5'09794'94--dc20   964488
                                                CIP

A Flame of Love martini toast to Maude Chasen and her beloved Dave and their wonderful restaurant where the stars dined.

To Armand Deutsch, who has accomplished many things in his extraordinary life. I am honored that producing this book was one of them. Without him, the true godfather of this project, it wouldn't have been possible.——B.G.

CONTENTS

INTRODUCTION

When Chasen's closed in 1995 after fifty-nine years of playing host to most all of its era's luminaries and thousands of others, it stood alone, and not just for its clientele. Chasen's had outlived all of the city's great old restaurants, including the Brown Derby, Romanoff's, La Rue, Perino's and Scandia. From the golden days of Hollywood, only the scrappy Musso & Frank Grill remains, a survivor since 1919.

No one can argue that changing times and changing tastes contributed to Chasen's demise. There was nothing remotely *nouvelle* about it. Toward the end, it became known as a place for the older generation, and their loyalty alone wasn't enough to drive it.

In this large restaurant there were only seventeen booths in two rooms that made a difference. History was made by the clientele seated in these best seats in the house — the ten booths in the "front room" and the seven in the adjoining "green room." (To be fair, in later years, when the bar was moved to the back of the restaurant, some power people actually preferred the privacy of the "bar room.") And if you weren't among the high and mighty, you knew it. A tuxedo-wearing maitre d' politely banished you to the great Siberia beyond. Such was the notorious pecking order.

In 1957, the *Saturday Evening Post* reported that Chasen's annual gross approached one million dollars. Its prosperity was no accident. Founder Dave Chasen, a poor Russian-Jewish immigrant born July 18, 1898, pushed hard seven days a week to turn his restaurant into something unique and successful. His one great indulgence was going fishing at Black Lake, Colorado, with his wife, Maude, and some of their famous friends for a week or two each year. Dave, of course, manned the stoves.

Odd as it may seem now, Chasen's first flourished at a time when a chef was secondary to a restaurant's owner. It wasn't until the 1970s that a Chasen's chef, Steno Rinaldi, emerged as something of a star, at least in print. In 1982 Bernard Klerlein took over the kitchen and kept that position until the restaurant closed for good.

Working with the Chasen family has been a joy. Their pride in Dave and Maude and the restaurant that bears their name is a rarity these days. They worked hard to be certain that the famous recipes, many of which had to be cut down from restaurant proportions, would be suitable for home cooking and taste delicious as well. They also want readers to know that, through the decades, Chasen's Chili has been a movable feast, with many chefs stirring the pot and adding their own subtle variations, as all chili makers do. The family is proud of the version in this book, as they are of each and every recipe.

After all, Chasen's history and its tastes are one, a remembrance of a once great establishment.

Chasen's

Chasen's as it appeared before its name change.

CHAPTER ONE

The Beginning

What do you think the odds would be that a baby born of poor parents in Odessa in southwest Russia in 1898 would one day wind up in Beverly Hills, California, rich, famous and loved by some of the most celebrated people on earth?

—Jimmy Stewart, 1973

It all really began in the 1920s on the vaudeville circuit. Dave Chasen was known not only as the mute stooge and second banana to comedian Joe Cook, but also for his gregarious and gentle personality and terrific backstage chili.

Cook was a big vaudeville star back then, up there with Al Jolson and Eddie Cantor. "He was a gentile Rube Goldberg," recalls Milton Berle, who shared the stage with Cook in 1919. Cook dealt with mechanical contraptions and went for visual gags —"humorously funny, not funny-funny," according to Berle.

Decked out in a red wig and blacked-out teeth, Dave was Cook's foil, the one destined to be clanked on the head with a ball that traveled through one of Cook's constructions of pipes and tubes. Dave never spoke. At the end of a bit, he signed off with a trademark gesture dubbed "The Idiot's Salute" that audiences waited for — a simpleton's smile followed by a slow wave of his right hand, palm facing the audience, across his face.

Cook discovered Dave and his wave on the circuit and hired him on the spot. Dave had emigrated as a child from Odessa, Russia, with his parents, Joseph and Alexis, who uprooted their family of five and settled in New Britain, Connecticut. Dave got into show business through a bit of clever marketing. When he was a teenager, he decided he wanted to fly and apprenticed himself to daredevil Charles K. Hamilton. By fifteen, he

Chasen's collection

Comedian Joe Cook, who discovered Dave Chasen on the vaudeville circuit.

was piloting his own plane. A subsequent crash closed that chapter of his flying career, but Dave came up with a scheme to charge audiences ten cents admission to view the wreckage and meet the surviving pilot at Keeney's Theatre in New Britain. When that attraction ran its course, Dave was hired to sit in the audience and heckle the comedian who was booked to perform after him. And so began his theatrical career.

Possibly because of the many late nights on the road when the players were reduced to eating cans of reheated beans, Dave developed another talent that would serve him well after vaudeville's — and Joe's — demise. He was always cooking up batches of chili in his dressing room for people in the company.

Thanks to a succession of Broadway smashes, including *George White Scandals*, *Earl Carroll Vanities*, *Fine and Dandy*, *Hold Your Horses* and *Rain or Shine*, the vaudeville comics became major attractions in Manhattan's theatrical social whirl. Many evenings after a show, literary lights such as *New Yorker* editor Harold Ross, critic Robert Benchley and playwright Marc Connelly congregated at Sleepless Hollow, Joe Cook's estate in Lake Hopatcong, New Jersey, for midnight feasts of barbecued ribs, steaks and chili prepared by Dave.

As vaudeville was dying, Cook and Dave appeared in the 1930 motion picture version of *Rain or Shine*, a hit directed by Frank Capra. Cook became fatally ill with Parkinson's disease soon after. Dave appeared in a few more pictures without Cook, but he must have realized that he was unlikely to make it in Hollywood.

Harold Ross admired Dave's culinary skills and was extremely fond of him personally. According to Capra, Dave approached the prestigious magazine editor with his restaurant idea, to which Ross replied, "Dave, you played the fool so long that now you want to be one. Don't you know that ninety-seven percent of all the blokes who start restaurants go bankrupt?"

Chasen's collection

Joe Cook (left) and a bewigged Dave were a winning team.

"I know it, Harold," his pal Dave returned, "but three percent don't."

Others say that it was the illustrious editor who planted the seed in Dave's mind, proposing that if he ever wanted to quit show business and open an eatery, Ross would put up the big money.

Whichever the case, Dave, who possessed a special quality for inspiring loyalty in people, borrowed a couple hundred dollars here and there from old friends. N.J. Blumberg, the former head buyer and booker for the Orpheum circuit who was now president of Universal Pictures, was one contributor. Capra lent him $200 and gave him the use of the fireplace at his Malibu home as his personal barbecue pit so Dave could fine-tune his recipes for ribs, sauce and chili. Ross put up the bulk of the money, initially investing $3,500 and persuading a friend, stockbroker Daniel Silverberg, to put up a smaller amount. Eventually Ross bought Silverberg out, and his total investment would soar over the next few years to approximately $20,000. It was a considerable sum, particularly for someone who wasn't rich and who had financial obligations to two ex-wives and a daughter.

Initially, Ross hoped that the restaurant would be located not in Hollywood but in Stamford, Connecticut, where he happened to be building a large home. "Of course, what we had in mind was a little place up in Connecticut near where we were living," Ross said. "You know, a place where we could all drop in and be sure of getting a solid meal." However, midway through negotiations to take over Chimney Corner, a failing restaurant on Long Ridge Road in North Stamford, it burned down.

Meanwhile, Ross's friend, vaudevillian Ed McNamara, visited Hollywood and reported back that there was no decent place to buy a steak in the town. So Dave changed directions.

Although there was nothing remotely Southern about the restaurant or Dave, Chasen's Southern Pit (Capra came up with the moniker) opened on December 13, 1936, at the corner of Doheny Drive and Beverly Boulevard, just east of the Beverly Hills border, where it would remain to the end. The original structure was barely big enough to house six tables, an eight-stool counter and a tiny kitchen. "It was what we call in Hollywood 'Mickey Mouse,' with three or four Ping-Pong tables outside," recalls the writer-director Billy Wilder, who attended the opening night party.

The only clue that the Southern Pit had arrived was a throwaway item in *The Hollywood Reporter*, the industry trade paper, buried beneath the

news that the James Cagneys were packing up to spend their Christmas in New York and that the McNaught Syndicate had signed up Will Rogers Jr. "Dave Chasen, who used to stooge for Joe Cook," the item read, was opening up his restaurant the next day with a cocktail party on the premises.

Wilder was recruited to attend the festivities by Sy Bartlett, a fellow writer at Paramount who knew Dave from New York. "I thought, why not? A free dinner. But it was very, very charming, and it was the best chili in town," Wilder said.

The bean field where Dave's glorified stucco shack stood proved an inspired choice, even though it must have seemed like the middle of nowhere at the time. Most of the town's swank gathering spots — the Brown Derby, the Biltmore Bowl, the Cocoanut Grove and Perino's — were situated further east in the Miracle

Mile district, in Hollywood and downtown Los Angeles. Dave's patch of land was a short spin from the palaces stars such as Mary Pickford and Douglas Fairbanks had erected in Beverly Hills. And it was just down the road from Cafe Trocadero, which had opened on the Sunset Strip in 1934, and not far from the posh twenty-four-year-old Beverly Hills Hotel and the newer Beverly Wilshire Hotel. Even if the Southern Pit wasn't any-

Chasen's collection

Dave was the head chef in the restaurant's tiny kitchen.

where near the movie studios, it was close to the talent agencies that were moving into the neighborhood. That included the important Music Corporation of America, precursor of MCA Inc., the parent of Universal Pictures. Lew Wasserman, who headed those companies, and his wife, Edie, became devoted customers. Besides dining there night after night and giving all their parties there, Wasserman made it a point early on to direct MCA agents to entertain their famous clients over dinner at Chasen's.

At first the menu consisted of barbecued spareribs (thirty-five cents), chili (twenty-five cents) and booze (thirty-five cents). By comparison, drinks ran from sixty cents to $1.50 at the posh Troc. Dave did the cooking, and he recalled years later, "When we were stuck for help, regulars like Lucille Capra would pitch in and wash dishes." *Colliers* reported that in the first days, Dave also had to pick up willing friends and bring them in to fill up tables. As of July, Silverberg fretted to Ross that a friend of his had been there for dinner and the place was empty.

Gradually, however, Chasen's business improved. East Coast exiles such as Nunnally Johnson, Charles MacArthur, James Thurber, Robert Benchley, Russel Crouse and Alexander Woollcott became regulars, no doubt on the urging of Ross. (Dorothy Parker should

get one free drink a day, Ross directed Dave.) Hollywood stars such as W.C. Fields, Spencer Tracy, Pat O'Brien and James Cagney, as well as Frank Capra, became fixtures. A John Decker portrait of Fields dressed as Queen Victoria became a permanent display at the restaurant's entrance.

It was, however, the kind of place where you didn't have to feel you were on display; early on, Dave instigated a policy of keeping photographers and gossip columnists away. Already it was more of a club than a restaurant. The stars' antics — with Ray Bolger dancing, Cagney and O'Brien breaking into song, Frank Morgan stripping and Fields playing table tennis with director Gregory La Cava until his dinner was ready — were becoming legend and putting the place on the map.

Within a few months, Dave enlarged the room and his menu, since patrons had begun to tire of a steady diet of chili and ribs. After Nunnally Johnson, for one, complained to Ross of "the sameness, or poverty, of our

In the beginning, Chasen's Southern Pit was a humble chili joint.

7

Hobo Steak

1 New York steak, at least 3 inches thick and large enough for 2 servings
fresh ground pepper
1 (¼-inch-thick) strip fat as wide as the steak is thick and long enough to encircle the steak, or several smaller strips of fat

1 cup salt
2 tablespoons water
2 slices (3x1½ x¼ -inch) toasted sourdough French bread
½ cup (1 stick) sweet butter

Season steak with pepper. Wrap fat strip around steak to cover sides completely, leaving the top and bottom uncovered. Note: Chasen's used the fat that was trimmed from the whole sirloin. Secure with one string near the top and another near the bottom. Tie another string over the steak. Combine salt and water to form a soft mush and mound on top of steak, completely covering meat.

Place steak about three inches below broiler flame and cook eight to ten minutes, depending on size, or until salt begins to separate or rise from meat. Remove salt crust, keeping crust in one piece. Flip steak and place salt on other side. Broil another eight to ten minutes. The meat should still be very rare.

Remove steak from oven, discarding salt, fat and string. Slice meat slightly on the diagonal. Heat butter in a chafing dish or large skillet until foaming and lightly browned. Place a few slices of meat at a time in foaming butter and cook about one minute on each side for rare meat or to desired degree of doneness. Place the steak slices on two pieces of toast and spoon some of the hot butter on top.

Serves two.

menu," the *New Yorker* editor wrote to Dave in one of his frequent missives: "If you're going to develop a hangout, which you already have on a considerable scale, to which people will go night after night, you've got to offer a greater variety so they won't get bored." The new, thirty-five-item menu included imported trout from Colorado, pompano from Florida, shrimp from New Orleans, oysters from Baltimore and even turbot from France.

One of the most popular dishes was Hobo Steak, a rich, salt-encrusted sirloin dish finished at the table, which Dave learned to make from fellow comic McNamara back in Lake Hopatcong. Dave said it came from the hobos' practice of packing their meat with mud to preserve its juices. The Hobo Steak would endure as a favorite for decades.

In the meantime, Ross was also pushing for a new name. In another letter, he suggested, "Call the place just 'Chasen's' or some such. Moreover, you're going to be more than a pit now, southern, eastern or arctic." A few days later, Ross reminded him, "What the hell does Southern Pit mean to anybody?" The novice restaurateur agreed to a name change but dragged his heels because his expensive neon sign was still brand-new. Finally, in 1940, the new, abbreviated designation — Chasen's — appeared on the restaurant's letterhead.

From left, regulars Bert Lahr, Herbert Marshall, Robert Benchley and David Niven dined in top form with Dave, at right.

CHAPTER TWO

The Golden Years

*Most successful restaurant owners make me feel like a worm with their superior-
ity, and accents, and ropes. But Chasen says, "Welcome, brother worm."*
                                    —Frank Capra, *Los Angeles Times*, August 26, 1973

By the war years, Chasen's had attained such a reputation as a
Hollywood hot spot that it was difficult to get a table. The biggest
stars of the day felt welcome there, including Charlie Chaplin,
William Powell, Robert Taylor, Joan Blondell and Dick Powell, James Cagney
("a very poor spender," Dave said), Ronald Colman, Leslie Howard and
Joan Bennett, as well as Joe DiMaggio, J. Edgar Hoover, oil magnate
William Keck, aircraft tycoon Donald Douglas and auto executives Ernie
Breech and K.T. Keller.

But the restaurant didn't owe its reputation solely to regular appearances
by the tycoons, movie stars and "ace executives and writers in movietown,"
as Dave called them. At Dave's insistence, the staff treated all customers to

top-drawer service.

"We used to joke that the parking lot was a used-Cadillac lot, but Dave said, 'Move the Fords in and get the Cadillacs off the lot. You cannot live on the motion picture business alone,'" said Tommy Gallagher, who joined Chasen's in 1947 as a waiter and became one of the captains in the prestigious front room.

The food was also considered superb. In the early 1940s, when the urbane actor Paul Henreid arrived in Hollywood, he proclaimed the town's food awful with three exceptions — Chasen's, Perino's and Romanoff's. Of the three, only Chasen's served primarily American cuisine. Perino's was a white-glove, European-style restaurant presided over by the courtly Alexander Perino and favored by Los Angeles society. Romanoff's, with its large Hollywood clientele, specialized in French cuisine and was run by a flamboyant former Chasen's waiter, "Prince" Michael Romanoff.

At Dave Chasen's kitchen you could take your pick from all-American to Jewish to Continental fare. In 1940 the menu featured chops, succotash and french-fried onions as well as gefilte fish and escargots. The barbecued ribs were history. Chili disappeared from the menu, but from then on, it and another signature dish, Deviled Beef Bones — breaded ribs made from the standing prime rib roast — would always be available by request for those in the know. Other restaurants discarded the ribs, but not Chasen's. However, you had to phone in your ribs order a week ahead, since one roast could only fill two orders.

Several other dishes, including Chicken Curry (a favorite of Frank Sinatra's) served with white rice or Rice a la Grecque, a colorful rice pilaf; Whitefish Portugaise, Creamed Spinach and Banana Shortcake — which Lucille Ball loved — became standards. A large repertoire of soups, including Tomato, Senegalaise, Petite Marmite and French Onion au Gratin, were also developed.

Dave virtually lived and breathed the restaurant. He had small quarters

Deviled Beef Bones

8 rib roast bones (detached from a previously roasted prime rib roast with some meat left on the bones)	1 cup yellow or English mustard 1 cup fine dry bread crumbs ¼ cup grated Parmesan cheese

Cut the bones apart. Place mustard in a shallow dish. In another dish, stir together bread crumbs and cheese. Dip the bones in mustard first to coat, then into bread crumb mixture until well coated. Place on a foil-lined baking sheet. Bake ribs about 30 to 40 minutes or until golden brown.

Serves four.

Chicken or Shrimp Curry

1½ pounds boneless, skinless
  chicken breasts
1 medium onion, thinly sliced
2 stalks celery, sliced
1 medium carrot, sliced
¼ teaspoon salt

¼ teaspoon pepper
1 cup dry white wine
2 cups heavy whipping cream
2 to 4 tablespoons Madras curry
  paste*
2 tablespoons all-purpose flour

Place chicken breasts in a Dutch oven with the onion, celery, carrots, salt and pepper. Add water to cover. Bring mixture to boil. Reduce heat, cover and simmer about 25 minutes or until chicken is no longer pink in the center. Transfer chicken to a plate to cool. Discard cooking liquid and vegetables.

Dice chicken into ¾-inch pieces. Return to Dutch oven with wine. Bring to boil. Reduce heat and simmer until reduced by half. Meanwhile, in a medium bowl stir together heavy whipping cream, curry paste and flour. Stir cream mixture into chicken. Cook and stir over medium heat until mixture thickens and bubbles. Simmer two minutes more, stirring constantly. Taste for seasoning. Serve curry mixture over rice pilaf. Serve with rice pilaf and curry condiments such as peanuts, raisins, shredded coconut and minced chives.

Serves four.

Variation: For Shrimp Curry, use 1½ pounds medium shrimp, shelled and deveined. Place in Dutch oven, eliminating chicken and vegetables. Boil shrimp in water until pink and drain. Return to Dutch oven with wine and continue as directed above.

*Madras curry paste is recommended. Use 2 tablespoons for moderately spicy curry, 4 tablespoons for a very spicy version.

there (his only residence) and started his days at 4 a.m. at the produce and meat markets. Although he now employed top chefs, he was always close to the kitchen. When the doors opened for dinner, he greeted guests in his trademark horn-rimmed glasses, bow tie and suit lined in red silk, a luxury he promised himself in his vaudeville days after admiring the red silk in a Chinese dance act. But even while he was greeting his friends at the booths, he had one eye on his staff. Recalls Ron Clint, who managed the restaurant for some thirty-five years, until it closed: "We'd do a party for 1,000 people. The next morning, we'd all be worn out. Dave would be in the kitchen holding up a celery stick saying, 'They put this in the wrong icebox and it turned black.'"

In the '40s, Chasen's earned a bicoastal reputation. Early on, a symbiotic relationship formed between Chasen's and "21", another clubby, American-style celebrity gathering place and Chasen's likely New York counterpart. Harold Ross was a habitué of "21", eating lunch there every other day, and Dave was fondly remembered as a "21" barfly from his acting days. "We loved David Chasen," said Jerry Berns, one of the owners of "21". "He was a down-to-earth chap and a very good restaurateur. We counted him almost as a member of the family. Anyone who said he was going to Los Angeles had a card of introduction to the "21" of Los Angeles. He would send people to us and we would send people to him."

Dave also dispatched some of his staff to "21" to observe how the floor was handled. At one point, Berns said, there were plans to bring "21" in as a partner in Chasen's, but the deal fell apart eventually.

Another acquaintance from Dave's acting days, Billy Grady Jr., a former Broadway agent, became one of

Rice a la Grecque

2 tablespoons butter
½ cup onion, minced
1 bay leaf
1 cup long grain rice
2 teaspoons chicken bouillon granules

2 cups water
½ cup cooked green peas
1 2-ounce jar diced pimentos, well-drained
3 tablespoons raisins

Melt butter in a deep 12-inch skillet. Saute onion and bay leaf over medium-low heat until onions are soft but not brown. Add rice, saute five minutes, stirring frequently. Stir in chicken bouillon and water. Bring mixture to boil. Cover tightly, reduce heat. Simmer 18 to 20 minutes or until liquid is absorbed and rice is fluffy. Remove bay leaf.

Stir in peas, drained pimentos and raisins. Cover and cook two minutes more.

Serves four to five.

Creamed Spinach

2 10-ounce packages frozen leaf spinach
  or 6 cups fresh washed spinach leaves,
  stems removed
water
2 tablespoons butter
2 tablespoons all-purpose flour

⅔ cup chicken broth
⅔ cup heavy whipping cream
¼ teaspoon lemon juice
¼ teaspoon Worcestershire sauce
salt and pepper to taste

If using frozen spinach, cook spinach according to package directions. For fresh spinach, pour one inch of water in a large heavy pot, bring to a boil. Add the fresh spinach and stir several times to cook evenly and until wilted.

Drain cooked spinach thoroughly, pressing out excess liquid with the back of a large spoon. Chop as desired or puree in a food processor.

Melt butter in a saucepan and stir in flour. Add broth and heavy cream all at once, stirring constantly over medium-high heat until mixture thickens. Stir in lemon juice and Worcestershire. Season to taste with salt and pepper. Combine thoroughly with well-drained spinach.

Serves six.

Chasen's most devoted customers. As head of casting at Metro-Goldwyn-Mayer, Grady was one of the most powerful figures in Hollywood, and, for decades, he had a six-days-a-week standing reservation. (Chasen's was closed on Mondays except for private parties.) To make sure he got the table he wanted, Grady enlisted studio carpenters to build his own booth along the wall outside one of the entrances to the front room. Grady thought of it as his own private office. "I did more business there, and I signed more actors in [Dave's]

place than anywhere else," Grady said. On the rare night he dined elsewhere, Grady made sure the patrons occupying his booth knew how fortunate they were. He hung his photograph there, along with a plaque reading: "You are

Chasen's collection

From left, Billy Grady Jr., Gloria and Jimmy Stewart gathered with Dave and Maude.

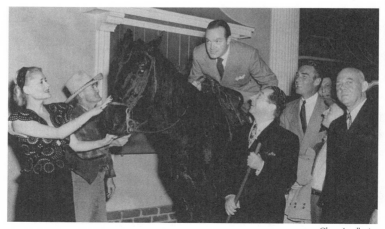

One of the most notorious stunts was Bob Hope's trot through Chasen's; Randolph Scott looks on in the background.

using this booth through the courtesy of Billy (Square Deal) Grady. P.S. But strictly on your own."

Grady's dinner companions naturally included stars such as Clark Gable and Mickey Rooney. But about four nights a week, his eating partner was Jimmy Stewart, whom Grady first brought out to Hollywood. Grady finally lost his dinner date when Stewart decided to marry Gloria Hatrick McLean, whom he, of course, courted at Chasen's. (To make a favorable impression on Gloria's imposing German shepherd, Stewart took him Chasen's steaks.) The night before their 1949 wedding, Dave hosted Stewart's bachelor party, one of Chasen's most memorable events. A sign out front announced, "Last Time Tonite — Jimmy Stewart — Farewell Appearance," and a German oompah band greeted guests.

Inside, Spencer Tracy, David Niven, Jack Benny, Lew Wasserman and others witnessed the moment when Stewart was asked to carve the roast. As he raised the lid of the silver platter, two diapered midgets jumped out, calling, "Daddy!"

Chasen's would become the Stewarts' lifelong home away from home, where Jimmy customarily dined on small amounts of thinly sliced Calf's Liver, smoked salmon or Hobo Steak. Joined eventually by their twin daughters, they dined there every Thursday night in the third booth to the left in the front room, beneath a photo of Jimmy as an eight-year-old. Dave's policy of leaving celebrities alone served well in the case of the reticent Stewart.

He was the least demanding of stars. "If he came in without a reservation, you could put him anywhere and he didn't care," said Clint. Chasen's also catered birthday parties at the Stewarts' home in Beverly Hills for the children.

Banana Shortcake

1 9 x 5-inch baked angel food, sponge
  or pound cake
1½ cups heavy cream, whipped
3 to 4 tablespoons granulated sugar

2 to 3 medium ripe bananas
Banana Sauce (see recipe below)
additional sliced bananas
hot fudge sauce

Slice the cake lengthwise into two layers. Place one layer on a serving platter. In a large bowl stir together the whipped cream and sugar to taste.

Spread some of the cream generously over the first cake layer. Peel bananas and lay them in a single layer over the cream. Spread more cream to cover bananas. Top with second cake layer. Frost top and sides of cake with remaining cream. (Cake may be prepared to this point several hours ahead of serving time; cover and chill until ready to serve.)

To serve cake, arrange some sliced bananas over top of cake. Slice cake crosswise into six pieces. Place each cake piece cut side down on plate. Top with Banana Sauce and hot fudge sauce.

Serves six.

Variation: For Strawberry Shortcake, hull and clean 1½ cups fresh strawberries, reserving six berries for garnish. Lay whole strawberries in place of bananas on first cake layer. Continue through frosting cake. Garnish top of cake with reserved berries. Then prepare Strawberry Sauce: Combine 1 cup chopped strawberries with sugar to taste. Puree in food processor. Serve cake with Strawberry Sauce and hot fudge sauce.

Banana Sauce

1 cup softened vanilla ice cream
½ cup heavy cream, whipped

1 banana, chopped
1 tablespoon dark rum (optional)

In a bowl stir together ice cream, whipped cream, chopped banana and rum, if desired, until well combined.

Tomato Soup

1 cup heavy cream
3 cups Tomato Sauce (see recipe, page 23)

salt and pepper to taste

In a heavy saucepan bring cream to a boil. Stir in Tomato Sauce; heat through. Season to taste with salt and pepper. Puree in food processor and serve.

Makes four servings.

Senegalaise Soup

2 tablespoons butter
½ cup leeks, sliced diagonally
½ cup onions, sliced
4 cups potatoes, diced
4 cups chicken broth
3 to 4 tablespoons Madras curry paste*

1 cup plus 3 tablespoons heavy whipping cream
1 teaspoon Worcestershire sauce
dash Tabasco sauce
salt and pepper to taste
minced fresh chives

Melt butter in a three-quart saucepan. Saute leeks and onions over low heat until tender but not browned. Add potatoes, cover with chicken broth. Bring mixture to a boil. Cover and reduce heat. Simmer 30 minutes or until potatoes are very tender. In a small bowl combine curry paste and 3 tablespoons heavy cream. Stir into potato mixture and bring to a boil. Remove from heat. Cool slightly. Puree mixture in food processor until very smooth.

Return mixture to saucepan. Stir in 1 cup heavy cream. Bring to a boil. Remove from heat. Stir in Worcestershire sauce, Tabasco, salt and pepper to taste.

Soup can be served hot or cold. Garnish hot soup with chopped chives. If you plan to serve it cold, cool the soup, then chill, covered, in the refrigerator.

Serves six.

*Madras curry paste is recommended. Use the smaller amount for medium hotness.

Petite Marmite Soup

3 cups chicken broth
1 cup beef broth
1 cup leeks, sliced diagonally

1 cup celery, sliced diagonally
1 cup carrots, sliced diagonally

Combine broths with vegetables in a large saucepan. Bring mixture to boil. Simmer about 15 minutes or until vegetables are tender.

Serves four.

French Onion Soup au Gratin

2 tablespoons butter
1½ cups onions, sliced
½ cup dry white wine
2½ cups beef broth
1½ cups chicken broth

½ teaspoon Worcestershire sauce
salt and pepper to taste
4 1-inch thick slices French bread
1 cup Monterey Jack cheese, shredded

Melt butter in a heavy three-quart saucepan. Saute onions over medium-low heat, stirring frequently, until deep golden brown. Stir in white wine. Simmer two minutes.

Stir in beef and chicken broths and bring to a boil. Reduce heat and simmer 10 minutes. Stir in Worcestershire sauce. Season to taste with salt and pepper.

Preheat broiler. Pour soup into four oven-proof crocks. Lay a slice of French bread on top of soup. Sprinkle cheese generously over bread. Broil until cheese is bubbly and lightly browned. Serve immediately.

Serves four.

Since Chasen's was populated by entertainers, it's not surprising that mischief-making was commonplace. Bob Hope rode through the front door on horseback, probably to promote his western farce *The Paleface* (1948). As a prank, Humphrey Bogart and Peter Lorre stole Dave's safe, only to discover it contained a bottle of brandy, which they proceeded to polish off.

Dave was almost always the most gracious and accommodating of hosts. Noticing that a pregnant Dorothy Lamour was having problems with her booth, he promptly sawed a portion out of table No. 12 to accommodate her.

Something exciting was always happening at the glamorous restaurant. When W.C. Fields' girlfriend,

Carlotta Monti, got wind that Fields was having dinner with another woman, Monti called Mount Sinai hospital to report that he was having a heart attack. An ambulance came and carried him away. Another time, Bogart, Clark Gable and Broderick Crawford got into a fistfight at the bar. The diminutive Dave was forced to throw Bogart off the premises bodily.

Quieter moments in the annals of Hollywood history occurred there too. Over dinner, William Wyler convinced David Niven to play Edgar in *Wuthering Heights*, even though Niven swore he'd never work with the "fiendish" director again. Subsisting entirely on Chasen's chow over a five-day period, Garson Kanin, his brother Michael and Ring Lardner wrote *Woman of the Year* — with Katharine Hepburn and two secretaries keeping them company — in Garson's villa at the Garden of Allah. Alfred Hitchcock outlined the plot of *Notorious* during a dinner at Chasen's with RKO producer William

Frank Sinatra, left, Ronald Reagan and Dave shared a drink.

Dozier. When he was portraying Charles Lindbergh in *The Spirit of St. Louis*, Jimmy Stewart invited the legendary hero to dinner in his booth. When word of Lindbergh's arrival got out, a battalion of photographers arrived. Lindbergh asked Dave to call for a taxi and made a quick exit.

Shirley Temple, at the height of her moppet fame, created a stir of her own when she began wailing the night her parents drank old-fashioneds before dinner. Temple said she wanted a drink of her own. "So we concocted,

---

Shirley Temple Cocktail

7-Up or ginger ale
grenadine
orange slice

maraschino cherry
toothpick

Fill tall glass with five parts 7-Up or ginger ale to one part grenadine. Garnish with an orange slice and a maraschino cherry on a toothpick.

A crowded evening included Jimmy Stewart towering over Groucho Marx, Alfred Hitchcock and Gloria Stewart.

that evening, on the spot, the original Shirley Temple cocktail — a touch of grenadine, a little fruit and lots of ginger ale," Dave recalled years later.

Hitchcock was the only other patron to be honored with an eponymous edible, although Dave respected his desire never to have Sole Hitchcock — sauteed imported Dover sole — added to the menu.

"The greatest gourmet, unquestionably, is Alfred Hitchcock. He and his wife, Alma, know their onions, literally," Dave told *Hollywood Reporter* columnist George Christy, then a food critic for *Los Angeles* magazine, in one of his last interviews.

In 1939, soon after he arrived in Hollywood from England to direct *Rebecca*, Hitchcock was introduced to Chasen's by Clark Gable and Carole Lombard. Hitchcock and his wife were so taken with Chasen's that their Thursday night dinners, always at booth No. 2 beneath a photograph of their daughter Patricia, became a

forty-year ritual. (Supposedly, in the early '50s, Hitchcock stayed away temporarily in order to lose weight before posing for *Rear Window* publicity pictures with Grace Kelly.) Hitchcock, who also relished the finest wines, was equally known at Chasen's for his habit of dozing off in the restaurant's comfortable booth.

Just about everyone who was anyone made at least one appearance nestled in one of Chasen's red or green leather booths. Greta Garbo reportedly made her first L.A. restaurant showing here. Regular Groucho Marx made it a practice to leave his hat and coat in his car, which he parked on the street, to avoid tipping the parking lot attendant and the hat check girl. Orson Welles was the biggest eater — ordering double orders of everything. Frank Sinatra, the smallest — ordering half orders. Howard Hughes, the simplest — typically dining on tomato juice, butterflied steak and salad.

In a position to increase the size of

Sole Hitchcock

4 8-ounce fillets of Dover sole
salt and pepper to taste
all-purpose flour as needed
2 whole eggs

4 tablespoons butter
cracker crumbs, as needed (Ritz or
  saltine)
Duglere sauce (see recipe below)

Preheat oven to 450 degrees. Clean, bone and trim fish. Season with salt and pepper. Coat fish with flour, dip in beaten eggs and coat with cracker crumbs. Shake off excess. In skillet over medium heat, saute fish in butter until golden brown on both sides. Place in preheated oven for ten minutes to finish cooking.

Remove from pan and transfer to a warm plate. Serve with Duglere Sauce.

Serves four.

Duglere Sauce

4 teaspoons butter
4 teaspoons shallots, minced
1 cup fresh tomatoes, chopped
salt and pepper to taste
1 tablespoon chives, minced

1 cup Chicken Cream Sauce
  (see recipe opposite)
2 tablespoons Tomato Sauce
  (see recipe opposite)

Heat butter in a heavy saucepan oven medium heat. Add shallots and tomatoes and saute until they are slightly softened. Season with salt and pepper. Add Chicken Cream and Tomato Sauces. Simmer. Sprinkle with chives and serve at room temperature.

Chicken Cream Sauce

3 tablespoons all-purpose flour
¼ cup chicken broth
½ cup heavy whipping cream

½ teaspoon lemon juice
½ teaspoon Worcestershire sauce
salt and pepper to taste

Melt the butter in a medium saucepan and stir in the flour. Stir in the broth and cream all at once. Cook and stir until mixture comes to a boil. Reduce heat, simmer two minutes more. Mix in lemon juice, Worcestershire sauce, salt and pepper to taste. Remove from heat.

Tomato Sauce

2 tablespoons butter
¼ cup onion, chopped
1½ cups tomato puree
1½ cups tomatoes, chopped
1 tablespoon fresh basil, minced

1 tablespoon fresh oregano,
 minced
½ teaspoon salt
¼ teaspoon pepper

Melt butter in a large skillet. Saute onion in butter until tender. Stir in tomato puree, chopped tomatoes, basil, oregano, salt and pepper. Simmer uncovered for 15 minutes over low heat or until reduced to desired consistency. Puree if desired. Makes about three cups.

Chasen's collection
Gracie Allen and George Burns at Chasen's.

Whitefish Portugaise

1½ pounds any white fish fillets
⅔ cup all-purpose flour
3 tablespoons olive oil
4 green pepper rings

4 small slices onion
4 slices tomato
salt and pepper to taste

Preheat broiler to 500 degrees or prepare grill (using a fish basket on the grill is recommended). Coat fish on all sides with flour, then dip in oil. Broil or grill fish on lightly greased pan or grate for about five minutes or until fish flakes easily. Meanwhile, place green pepper rings in oiled pan. Place one onion ring inside each bell pepper ring. Top each with a tomato slice. Broil or grill each vegetable stack for several minutes until warmed through. Carefully place a vegetable stack on top of each serving of fish. Season to taste.

Serves four.

his staff, Dave hired a fellow Russian immigrant who had hitchhiked to California from New York. Harold

Chasen's collection

Don Ameche was responsible for introducing Dave to Maude.

Ross had written Dave to say that, as a publicity stunt, he hired Michael Romanoff, an amusing chap with an English accent, to serve as assistant and host. "Possibly after spending a few days in a few jails on the way, Mike will show up out there sooner or later," Ross wrote. "He says he's willing to grab an apron and get to work. . . If he gets pinched in the place, it won't do it any harm. Mike had his tailcoat and white tie outfit out of hock the night we were with him and that's what gave us the idea of sending him out."

The engaging Romanoff professed to be a Russian prince. Movie people, whether or not they believed his story, found him entertaining. At first, when Romanoff started lining up wealthy customers to invest in a restaurant of his own, Dave didn't protest. He figured people could go to Romanoff's place for lunch, when Chasen's was

Danny and Sylvia Kaye hobnobbed with Dave.

closed, and come to his restaurant for dinner. But when he caught Romanoff on the sidewalk in front the restaurant trying to hire his waiters and captains, Dave punched him and broke his jaw. Romanoff's opened in 1941 in Beverly Hills, where it remained for twenty-one years, and the two restaurateurs didn't speak to each other for twenty of them.

Chasen's grew like topsy, dining room by dining room, and at various times, it included a barber shop and TV room. There was a steam room and shower, so actors and others arriving from the east could come directly from the train station or airport, refresh themselves, have a good meal and then go home. Dave had an extra locker for nonregulars that he labeled "Josephine Baker."

Dave hated having to turn people away when they called and asked, "Can you handle 350?" so he kept

enlarging — and buying pieces of land, eventually taking over the entire, enormous corner. In 1942, when the expanded men's bathroom was completed, Nunnally Johnson took it upon himself to stage a Hollywood-style premiere, heralding the evening with truckloads of flowers and klieg lights.

When James Thurber surprised Dave with a sexy mural sketched in charcoal in the men's room, Dave was thrilled. "It was a brilliant piece of erotic art. I planned to have it varnished for posterity the next day," Dave said. The following morning, however, a cleaning woman told him: "Some drunk scribbled all over the walls in there, Mr. Chasen, but I worked all night and washed 'em off."

Throughout the '40s, business boomed. Ross had earned more than $200,000 on his investment, representing a substantial portion of his wealth, when he made arrangements

Gallagher Family collection

Serviceman Elvis Presley waited to be served by Tommy Gallagher.

Calf's Liver

1½ pounds calf's liver
salt and pepper to taste

½ cup all-purpose flour
3 tablespoons olive oil or butter

Slice liver diagonally into ¼-inch-thick slices. Season to taste with salt and pepper. Coat pieces with flour on both sides.

Heat oil or butter in a large skillet until medium hot. Saute liver on both sides until browned and slightly firm to the touch. Do not overcook or use high heat.

As an alternative method of preparation, dip slices in oil, place under broiler and cook to desired doneness.

Serve with sauteed onions, bacon and mashed potatoes.

Serves four.

to turn his shares over to Dave. Ross no longer felt it was right to profit from Dave's hard work. He and Dave drew up the papers that would return Ross's shares to Dave in 1953, including a clause specifying that if Ross died before then, the shares would auto-matically go to Dave. Ross died prematurely in 1951.

Long before Dave lost one partner, however, he acquired another. In 1941 Don and Honey Ameche introduced him to a gorgeous blond Southern belle, Maude King Martin.

Dave had been divorced after a brief, early marriage. Then for years he had been married to the restaurant, living in his windowless room. The Ameches made it a point to take their house guest from New York to Chasen's for nightcaps during her Los Angeles vacation. They would be joined there, of course, by Dave.

Based in New York City, Maude supervised all the hair salons in Saks Fifth Avenue stores across the country. Divorced and the mother of a young daughter, Kay, she had supported herself first as a school teacher, then in various department stores' cosmetics departments. She eventually rose through the ranks of Seligman & Latz, which ran salon concessions at department stores around the country, including Saks. She spent three months every summer in Paris to be with Saks' star stylist, Antoine, and was at the top of her profession when she decided she wanted to move to Los Angeles — but not for Dave. Her first impression, she told the Ameches, was that Dave "certainly wasn't tall, dark and handsome." But after her vacation, she was definitely attracted to Los Angeles and wanted to move. If Seligman & Latz could give her a job, fine, if not, she'd quit. Appointed manager of L.A.'s May Company store salons, she bought a house in nearby Westwood.

Once in Los Angeles, she began seeing Dave regularly, joining him for dinner at table No. 5. "Dave would be forever popping up and down. That's how they did their courting," says Kay.

The couple was married in Las

Academy of Motion Picture Arts and Sciences

Elizabeth Taylor and Eddie Fisher at Chasen's premiere party for "Suddenly Last Summer" in 1959.

Vegas on September 13, 1942 — 13 for the date when Chasen's opened, Dave's lucky number. They honeymooned at Ross's Connecticut house. Soon after their return to Los Angeles, Dave received his draft notice. With no one to run the business, he might be forced to sell and all he could get at the time would be five cents on the dollar. Given a brief extension, Dave turned to the sharp businesswoman at his side and taught her how to run Chasen's.

It turned out, though, that Dave spent only one day in service at Fort MacArthur. The army changed its age limit — all of a sudden, he was too old to serve.

To Maude's joy, "Dave came marching home.

While playing the title role in "Cleopatra," Elizabeth Taylor made Chasen's Chili world famous when she had it shipped to Rome.

CHAPTER THREE

Chasen's Chili

Dear Dave, please send me ten quarts of your wonderful chili in dry ice.

—Elizabeth Taylor, on location in Rome, 1962

In the annals of chili history, there is probably no chili more famous than Chasen's Chili. Whether or not you liked it — and Chasen's Chili had its detractors among chili aficionados of the world — it was as celebrated as a pot of beans, beef and spices can be.

The marvel wasn't that Dave, back in his various kitchenettes on the vaudeville circuit, attained the right proportion of ingredients to gladden most people's stomachs. It was that after his little shack on Beverly Boulevard evolved into one of the most elegant restaurants in the United States, he kept serving this, the humblest of foods, a dish that is believed to have been cooked first by ranch hands in San Antonio, Texas.

"We never got too fancy for chili," said Dave plainly.

"There was something wonderfully nutty about an upscale restaurant like Chasen's being famous for a downscale dish," said Los Angeles food critic Merrill Shindler. "It's like Spago being best known for its pizza. It gave the place a great deal of humanity."

Jack Benny ordered it by the quart. J. Edgar Hoover considered it the best chili in the world. Eleanor Roosevelt sought but was refused the closely guarded recipe (a complimentary order was dispatched to her instead). But it was Elizabeth Taylor, while playing the title role of the epic movie *Cleopatra*, who made Chasen's Chili world famous.

In 1962, during the filming of the movie in Rome, the headline-making star presumably tired of Italian fare. She so much craved Chasen's Chili that she was willing to pay $100 just to have an order shipped to her. Hedda Hopper reported that Taylor couldn't live without the chili, even though, the columnist sniped, "It's not exactly Metrecal, so Liz had a time squeezing into the Cleo costumes, but it kept her fat and happy."

Privately, Maude always told family and friends that she believed Taylor, then married to Eddie Fisher, snagged her co-star Richard Burton with the rich, full-bodied chili. In any case, Taylor apparently was on cloud nine, as she wrote to Dave, "We cannot tell you what your chili has done for us all the way over here. Like that Jewish song, 'Sure and a little bit of heaven fell out of the sky one day.'"

Dave kept the recipe a secret, entrusting it to no one. For years, he came to the restaurant every Sunday to privately cook up a batch, which he would freeze for the week, believing that the chili was best when reheated. "It is a kind of bastard chili" was all that he would divulge.

Dave wanted to can and market his chili and even printed labels.

30

THE WHITE HOUSE

WASHINGTON

**The Western White House
San Clemente**

July 12, 1972

PERSONAL

Dear Mrs. Chasen:

This is just a note to thank you for arranging
to send the delicious chili to San Clemente -
as you suggested, I did share it with Henry
Kissinger and Bebe Rebozo, and we all
thoroughly enjoyed it.

I also appreciated receiving the recipes for
some of my favorite dishes.

With best wishes,

Sincerely,

Richard Nixon

Mrs. Maude Chasen
Chasen's
9039 Beverly Boulevard
Los Angeles, California 90048

President Richard Nixon was one of the restaurant's biggest chili fans. *Chasen's collection*

Even before Elizabeth Taylor placed her order, demand was so great that Dave set out to can the chili for nationwide distribution. He got as far as printing the labels, but his plan was stymied by problems with the canning process.

Renowned chili connoisseur Frank X. Tolbert in his authoritative book *A Bowl of Red* maintained that Chasen's Chili would receive only a "passing grade" from a true chili buff. In Tolbert's opinion, it was merely a fine "stew." True Texas chili would never include tomato, green pepper or onion as Chasen's Chili did.

Nevertheless, many gourmets, including Jeanne Voltz, the food editor of the *Los Angeles Times* from 1960 to 1972, considered it a "classic chili" —

Chili

½ pound dried pinto beans	2 pounds beef chuck, coarsely
water	chopped*
1 28-ounce can diced tomatoes in juice	1 pound pork shoulder, coarsely
1 large green bell pepper, chopped	chopped*
2 tablespoons vegetable oil	⅓ cup Gebhardt's chili powder
3 cups onions, coarsely chopped	1 tablespoon salt
2 cloves garlic, crushed	1½ teaspoons pepper
½ cup parsley, chopped	1½ teaspoons Farmer Brothers
½ cup butter	ground cumin**

Rinse the beans, picking out debris. Place beans in a Dutch oven with water to cover. Boil for two minutes. Remove from heat. Cover and let stand one hour. Drain off liquid.

Rinse beans again. Add enough fresh water to cover beans. Bring mixture to a boil. Reduce heat and simmer, covered, for one hour or until tender.

Stir in tomatoes and their juice. Simmer five minutes. In a large skillet saute bell pepper in oil for five minutes. Add onion and cook until tender, stirring frequently. Stir in the garlic and parsley. Add mixture to bean mixture. Using the same skillet, melt the butter and saute beef and pork chuck until browned. Drain. Add to bean mixture along with the chili powder, salt, pepper and cumin.

Bring mixture to a boil. Reduce heat. Simmer, covered, for one hour. Uncover and cook 30 minutes more or to desired consistency. Chili shouldn't be too thick — it should be somewhat liquid but not runny like soup. Skim off excess fat and serve.

Makes 10 cups, or six main dish servings.

*Chasen's used the best beef chuck, center cut, trimmed completely of fat. The restaurant used a special meat grinder, but for the home cook, meat chopped into one-quarter to one-half-inch chunks is much better than ground meat for this chili.

**Sometimes cumin seed is used in place of the ground cumin. It's a matter of personal preference.

Note: You can freeze this chili for several months. When reheating refrigerated leftover or frozen chili, add a few tablespoons of water to regain proper consistency.

not as spicy as most Texas chilis, but spicy enough. "It wasn't very heavy on tomatoes. They used good meat, which they knew how to buy. It was a well-balanced dish," Voltz said.

"There is no 'right' chili," opined Shindler, "but chili people tend to be that way. It's just your classic, good, thick, rich chili. It was one of those perfect culinary moments."

A variation was Chili Mac — Chasen's Chili served over spaghetti.

Chili Mac

8 ounces uncooked spaghetti   ¼ cup shredded sharp Cheddar cheese
4 cups Chili (see recipe opposite)

Cook spaghetti in a large pot of salted boiling water until nearly tender (*al dente*). Drain.

Preheat boiler. Divide spaghetti among four oven-proof au gratin dishes. Spoon chili over pasta. Sprinkle with the cheese. Place under the broiler until cheese melts. Serve with Cheese Toast (see recipe, page 51) and chopped onions.

Serves four.

Courtesy Ronald Reagan Presidential Library

President Ronald Reagan lined up for a helping of Chasen's chili at his ranch.

Dave, consultant and caterer to TWA, and Maude posed in an advertisement for the Jetstream with "silver service."

CHAPTER FOUR

Chasen's To Go

All the Hollywood people used Chasen's.
—Terry Stanfill, 1995

Spencer Tracy and his wife dined at Chasen's one or two nights a week. But when Tracy was at Katharine Hepburn's house, Chasen's dinners were delivered to them personally by captain Tommy Gallagher. Almost from the start, it was possible to enjoy a Chasen's meal outside the restaurant. Dave realized that expanding his horizons would be profitable. In 1938 he entered a partnership with Saks Fifth Avenue to operate the Terrace Snack Bar at the company's gleaming new store on Wilshire Boulevard in Beverly Hills. The roof-top restaurant appealed to weary shoppers with luncheon, tea and cocktails served in a serene rock fountain and garden setting. Dave acted as host of "Chasen's Atop Saks Fifth Avenue," as a 1942 Chasen's menu promoted the restaurant. Concessions followed at Caliente race track in Tijuana and El

Capitan Theatre in Hollywood. After his release from the army, Dave was also put to work feeding thousands at an air base near San Bernardino and at an air procurement center in Los Angeles. He even ran a small restaurant at the Albuquerque Airport for a few years.

When Howard Hughes bought Transcontinental and Western Air in 1939 (the precursor to Trans World Airlines), he asked Dave to make it the first airline to serve passengers hot meals — on good china and linens — instead of the usual boxed sandwiches. Hughes ate at Chasen's often and usually spent half the night in Dave's office making phone calls. Dave had some experience preparing in-flight meals since another fan of Dave's food, Albuquerque resident and Continental Airlines president Robert Six, had

already asked him to make chicken sandwiches for his passengers.

For TWA, Dave had to figure out a way to prepare the food at Chasen's and keep it warm on its way to the airport. He mastered the problem through trial and error, using trucks equipped with heating devices.

Dave was on board when Hughes personally piloted some of his famous friends to New York on a Constellation. The starry passenger list included Cary Grant, William and Diana "Mousie" Powell, Paulette Goddard and Burgess Meredith. About ten minutes before landing, the plane dropped 20,000 feet because of inclement weather and flailing winds. When Hughes asked for a drink, his passengers grew even more alarmed because Hughes was a teetotaler. Dave brought forth an eighty-five-year-old bottle of

The catering staff paused for a photo at Vera and N. J. Blumberg's twenty-fifth anniversary party.

vodka. To Dave's horror, Hughes poured the entire bottle on a piece of cloth and used it to wipe the condensation from the windshield.

Ultimately, the assignment of supplying gourmet meals for TWA became too big and Dave bowed out. However, he consulted for the airline until the end of his life. Hughes selected Chasen's, of course, to cater the party for the launch of the Spruce Goose, for its one and only flight on November 2, 1947.

Once the restaurant had a small battalion of catering trucks, it was only natural that Chasen's would develop a full-scale private catering operation. The timing couldn't have been better. The movie industry was booming, and entertaining on a grand scale was important to its image. There was little competition in the business of nourishing large, glamorous, class-A Hollywood parties, much less small, intimate ones. If someone's chef walked out, or if it was the cook's night off, Dave could easily send over dinner for two or twelve, pronto.

Dave knew a golden opportunity when he saw it. In 1946, one of Chasen's biggest jobs was the twenty-fifth wedding anniversary party for 600 for Universal Pictures president N.J. Blumberg and his wife, Vera. It was held on the tent-enveloped tennis court of the Blumbergs' estate in Sherman Oaks. That affair was followed a year later by their daughter Doris's wedding on the same court. And so it went. By the end of the '40s, Chasen's was catering a party a week, and Dave had the whole thing down to a science. For every six guests there would be seven feet of space "so they'll be packed firmly but not uncomfortably," he said, and tennis courts proved ideal. He also estimated that between the hours of 7 p.m. and 4 a.m., the average party-goer consumed five glasses of champagne. Chasen's took care of every detail under the

Gallagher Family collection

Chasen's catering crew brought dinner to Joan Crawford's home in the restaurant's signature crate, right.

Mustard Sauce

1 medium Bermuda onion	2 teaspoons Worcestershire sauce
½ teaspoon dry mustard such as Colman's	¼ teaspoon freshly ground pepper
1 tablespoon prepared French mustard	4 tablespoons mayonnaise

Grate onion. Place in center of linen napkin, squeeze out and reserve all juice. Combine onion juice and dry mustard. Blend into paste. Add prepared mustard and Worcestershire sauce. Sprinkle pepper over mayonnaise. Add to first mixture. Blend all ingredients thoroughly. Serve with cold seafood such as fresh crab meat.

Serves four.

tent — lighting, flowers, party favors, carved ice sculptures, hat check racks and, of course, hat check girls.

Alfred Hitchcock hosted some of the most unique Chasen's off-site parties. One Halloween, the director served black water and staged a fight between chefs who ended up soaked with fake blood. But Hitchcock could also be quite refined. Once he had a sit-down dinner for 150 at which each person was seated at his own table.

Chasen's undertook some of the most massive catering assignments of the day — and some of the most important dinners in Los Angeles, from a sit-down dinner for 3,000 guests during the 1960 Democratic National Convention to post-movie premiere suppers for *West Side Story, Julia, Saturday Night Fever* and many others. Dennis Stanfill, former 20th Century Fox Studio head and his wife, Terry, hosted many dinner parties for Fox's board of directors, including Princess Grace of Monaco, at which Chasen's food was served.

Other royalty who have dined on Chasen's chow include Charles, the Prince of Wales, over lunch at Fox studios; Sweden's King Carl Gustaf XVI, feted at a Western-style barbecue which took place on the Warner Bros. lot with Edgar Bergen and Charlie McCarthy entertaining the king; and Britain's Princess Margaret and Lord Snowdon, guests of MCA-founder Jules Stein at Universal.

The 1979 preview of the new Neiman Marcus store in Beverly Hills, a fundraiser for the Los Angeles Music Center, was one of Chasen's most challenging assignments. A different course was served on each of the store's four floors. Dinner began in the shoe department with cold seafood on ice accompanied with Chasen's famous Mustard Sauce, progressed upward with steak tartare, roast beef, chili and dessert. It was one of the rare occasions, though, when Chasen's Chili was supplanted by Neiman

Marcus' own Red River Chili. Among the 2,300 diners riding the escalators for the next course were California Governor Edmund G. "Jerry" Brown Jr., conductor Zubin Mehta, Stanley Marcus and Music Center founder Dorothy Chandler.

In 1983, First Lady Nancy Reagan and 500 members of Los Angeles' social royalty — Cary Grant, Fred Astaire, Ginger Rogers, Gene Kelly, Bette Davis and Frank Sinatra as well as the Bill Dohenys, Walter Annenbergs and Paul Trousdales — feted Britain's Queen Elizabeth II and her husband, Prince Philip, at a down-home, though formal-dress, Chasen's bash on the M*A*S*H soundstage at 20th Century Fox. "Mrs. Reagan kept it simple," Ron Clint recalled of the unusual menu. "That's the way her dinners were." After a first course of papaya with bay shrimp, out came piping-hot, individual Chicken Pot Pies (the queen ate every morsel of hers, according to Clint, who checked), Spinach with Bacon and Coupe Snowballs for dessert.

Maude was responsible for adding Chicken Pot Pie to Chasen's repertoire. The hearty Sunday special, chock-full of chicken and vegetables, became one of Chasen's signature dishes and one of its most popular. Maude said her grandmother taught her to make it over a Georgia wood and coal stove. "She would make me make it over and over until I got it right," Maude once recalled.

When the cost of catering skyrocketed and competitors entered the fray, Dave began adding more banquet rooms. "He said, 'To heck with you,'" Clint said. Rather than take Chasen's to the parties, the parties came to Chasen's.

Through the years, though, Hollywood's most legendary party givers continued to throw glorious bashes at home or at their movie studios, where tables groaned with provisions from Chasen's. Oil man and one-time 20th Century Fox studio owner Marvin Davis and his wife, Barbara; Cubby and Dana Broccoli, he the producer of the James Bond movies and grandson of the vegetable developer ("Yes, we had to have broccoli," said Clint); producer Jerry Weintraub and his wife, Jane Morgan; and Lew and Edie Wasserman

Lewis F. Blumberg collection

Producer Walter Wanger, left, Joan Bennett and producer-studio executive William Goetz at the Blumberg anniversary party.

Courtesy Ronald Reagan Presidential Library

*In 1983, First Lady Nancy Reagan welcomed Queen Elizabeth II
to 20th Century Fox for a dinner in Her Majesty's honor.*

hosted some of the grandest affairs. There were also spectacular fundraising dinners for the Huntington Library, SHARE, the Amazing Blue Ribbon 400 of the Music Center and other important charities at various locations around town.

Chasen's also continued its practice of food to go on a small scale. When a good patron was admitted to a local hospital (Mount Sinai Hospital, which later became Cedars-Sinai Medical Center, was conveniently located across the street in those days),whether for childbirth or surgery, Dave and Maude always sent over a complimentary dinner. On one particularly sad occasion, a Chasen's waiter delivered a dinner to Clark Gable at Good Samaritan Hospital. On the drive back to the restaurant, the waiter heard a flash on the radio announcing that the beloved actor had just died.

Chicken Pot Pie

Makes one 9-inch pie or six individual pies

3 whole chicken breasts
6 chicken thighs*
1 medium onion, sliced
2 stalks celery, sliced
1 medium carrot, sliced
¼ teaspoon salt
¼ teaspoon pepper
Chicken Cream Sauce
  (see recipe, page 23)

1 cup baby carrots, trimmed and quartered,
  boiled until almost tender
1 cup frozen green peas, thawed
1 cup new potatoes, quartered and boiled
  until almost tender
½ cup pearl onions, blanched for 1 minute
pastry for a 9-inch one-crust pie, or one
  sheet frozen puff pastry, thawed
1 egg yolk
1 teaspoon water

Place chicken, onion, celery, carrot, salt and pepper in a Dutch oven, cover with water. Cover and bring to boil. Reduce heat, simmer covered for 25 minutes or until chicken is no longer pink. Remove chicken and cool. Strain broth and set aside to use in Chicken Cream Sauce.

Preheat oven to 425 degrees. Discard bones and cut chicken into medium-sized pieces. Place chicken evenly in bake-and-serve dish. (If using a traditional pie dough, divide between 6 individual souffle dishes, or soup crocks or a 9-inch deep-dish pie pan. If using sheets of puff pastry, use a 12 x 8 x 2-inch rectangular baking dish.) Sprinkle with quartered carrots, peas, potatoes and pearl onions. Pour sauce evenly over chicken and vegetables. Crust will be used on top of pie only. Place pie dough over filling, crimping edges, or lay puff pastry over chicken and vegetables, trimming at edges of pan if necessary. Cut a few slits in the pastry to allow for steam to escape. Beat together egg yolk and water. Brush mixture over crust.

Bake for 25 to 30 minutes or until pastry is golden brown and filling is bubbly. Let stand five minutes before cutting.

Serves six.

Variation: You can make this pie with a traditional pie pastry crust or a puff pastry crust. For individual pot pies, (you'll need pastry for a double-crust pie to make six individual round tops or cut puff pastry into six rectangles to fit on top of au gratin dishes.

*At Chasen's the dark meat was left on the bone.

Spinach Salad with Bacon

1½ bunches fresh spinach
⅓ cup bacon, cooked crisp and chopped
½ cup fresh mushrooms

½ cup French Dressing
  (see recipe below)
½ tablespoon red wine vinegar
¼ teaspoon Worcestershire sauce
freshly ground pepper to taste

Remove stems and wash spinach leaves in several changes of cold water until there is no trace of sand. Dry well and chill in refrigerator. Wash the mushrooms and dry them well. Trim off the bottom of the stems and discard. Thinly slice mushrooms. Combine the red wine vinegar and Worcestershire sauce with the French dressing in a cup. Place the spinach in a large bowl. Tear large leaves into smaller pieces. Add the mushrooms, dressing and bacon. Toss to mix thoroughly. Sprinkle with freshly ground pepper. Serve on chilled plates.

Makes four servings.

French Dressing

1 teaspoon sugar
1 teaspoon salt
¼ teaspoon pepper
¼ teaspoon dry English mustard
¼ cup red wine vinegar
¾ cup olive oil

½ cup vegetable oil
1 teaspoon lemon juice
½ teaspoon Worcestershire sauce
1 clove garlic, finely chopped
¼ teaspoon Tabasco sauce
⅛ teaspoon white pepper

In a shaker dissolve sugar, salt, pepper and English mustard in vinegar. Add oils, lemon juice, Worcestershire, garlic, Tabasco and white pepper. Cover and shake vigorously. Set aside or chill until needed.

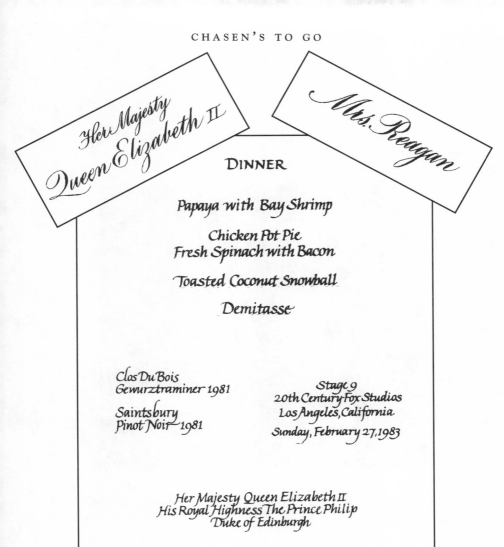

Her Majesty Queen Elizabeth II

Mrs. Reagan

DINNER

Papaya with Bay Shrimp

Chicken Pot Pie
Fresh Spinach with Bacon

Toasted Coconut Snowball

Demitasse

Clos Du Bois
Gewurztraminer 1981

Saintsbury
Pinot Noir 1981

Stage 9
20th Century Fox Studios
Los Angeles, California

Sunday, February 27, 1983

Her Majesty Queen Elizabeth II
His Royal Highness The Prince Philip
Duke of Edinburgh

Ron Clint collection

Place cards, top, and menu commemorate the dinner hosted by First Lady Nancy Reagan honoring Queen Elizabeth II and Prince Philip.

43

From left, Fred MacMurray, June Haver and "This Is Your Life"'s Ralph Edwards celebrate with Dave after the television show.

CHAPTER FIVE

The Sixties and Beyond

Chasen's was always important, society-wise. It felt like a club, just like "21" in New York or the Jockey Club in Washington.
— **Wolfgang Puck, 1995**

By the '60s Chasen's had become an institution. In 1961 it won *Holiday* magazine's tenth annual restaurant award (along with Los Angeles's Perino's, Scandia and La Rue), and Ralph Edwards surprised an unsuspecting Dave on his television show, *This Is Your Life*. Dave's good friends Jane Wyman, Fred MacMurray, Mervyn LeRoy and Billy Grady Jr. assembled for the telecast along with his two siblings, including brother Phillip, who worked behind the scenes at Chasen's.

Reflecting on his success, Dave credited Chasen's cuisine. "In the restaurant business, don't let anybody fool you — the food is still the thing."

"Chasen's was very American in a meat-and-potatoes way, but it wasn't just any old meat. It was very fine American food and very fine American-style service," remembers Jeanne Voltz of the *Los Angeles Times*. Indeed, Chasen's was staunchly traditional in many ways. A coat-and-tie dress code for men remained in place (relaxed only for Groucho Marx and his turtle-necks) even when jeans and Gucci loafers became the local uniform. In fact, it wasn't until the energy crisis of the early '70s forced the restaurant to reduce its air conditioning that men were allowed to dine tieless.

Though it was the age of plastic, Chasen's was unique in keeping credit cards off limits. Many first-timers often "went white with fear," Ron Clint confirmed, when they were apprised of the unusual policy, which continued right up to the mid-1980s. From the start, though, Dave offered "house accounts" to customers, which he considered "a friendlier way" of payment than cash or check, which were also accepted. There were some 8,000 house accounts on file, and few

deadbeats among them. Among those Dave reportedly delayed billing was George Raft during a period when the actor was experiencing tax trouble. "No matter how often I've treated stars to meals because they were having money trouble, they always paid me back later," he observed.

Since the restaurant was never a white-wine-and-sparkling-water type of enterprise, it was also fitting that bartender Pepe Ruiz concocted a mixed drink for Dean Martin that quickly joined the ranks of Chasen's standards. As a change of pace from the traditional martinis Martin sipped at the bar three or four nights a week, Ruiz spiked one with La Iña sherry. The cocktail was dubbed Flame of Love because it was polished off with a flambe of orange peel. Martin "went crazy" over it, Ruiz said.

In 1967, Dave and Maude cele-brated their twenty-fifth wedding anniversary with a bash at their Hollywood Hills home. The event brought forth the notables who con-tributed to the restaurant's fame — Groucho Marx, Jimmy Durante, Greer Garson, producer-director Hal Roach, the Fred MacMurrays, Ann Miller, the Jimmy Stewarts, the Alfred Hitchcocks, Mrs. Clark Gable, Billy Grady Jr. and Continental Airlines tycoon Robert Six and his wife, Audrey Meadows. Columnist Earl Wilson and his wife, B.W., who hosted

Chasen's collection

From left, Felicia Farr, Jimmy Stewart and Jack Lemmon join Dave at his and Maude's twenty-fifth anniversary party.

the Chasens' tenth anniversary party, flew out from New York for the evening. They all talked about the old days and consumed the dish that got the whole thing started, Chasen's Chili, along with a spread that included rack of lamb, salmon and fillet of beef. Now a glamorous grandmother of three, Maude danced with her guests until midnight.

In the early '70s Dave considered opening a second, smaller restaurant in Palm Springs, where he and Maude owned a second home. It was a notion entertained only briefly. Dave was aware that Romanoff's on the Rocks in Palm Springs had been a financial disaster for his rival, Mike Romanoff, earlier and had contributed to the closing of the famous Beverly Hills restaurant in 1962.

After Dave was diagnosed with cancer in 1968, he was forced to take a less active role at Chasen's and gradually turned over responsibility for it to Maude. She had always overseen remodeling and redecorating as the restaurant grew, but now her role enlarged considerably. Up to that point, she explained, "I wasn't very visible in the restaurant. He wanted me to be, but I always felt he was the star, so I worked mainly behind the scenes on the finances and keeping up the decor." Of course, Maude was certainly a familiar presence. There was a Maude's Salad on the menu — a light, chopped appetizer salad served with Roquefort dressing — and there was a salad named for daughter Kay, made with string beans and onion. But as Dave's health declined, Maude moved up front and transformed herself into Chasen's elegant hostess.

"She adored her new role," said Maude's good friend Walter Boxer. "She would 'do the tables,' as I called it, saying hello to the regulars. From her experience in the beauty business, she was an aggressive businesswoman with foresight, adding the back patio and the California banquet

Flame of Love Martini

a few drops of La Iña sherry
2 thick strips of orange peel

1½ ounces vodka or gin
ice

Swirl a few drops of sherry in a chilled, stemmed glass and pour out. Squeeze strip of orange peel in the glass and flambe with a match so that the bouquet from the orange peel fills the glass. Discard peel. Fill glass with ice. Add vodka or gin and flambe the second piece of orange peel. Discard peel. Stir.

Serves one.

Maude, in Dave's photograph-lined office, carried on the Chasen's tradition after Dave's death.

room when new competition came to town."

By the 1970s, Los Angeles had experienced the invasion of the French. Celebrity haunts, such as the Bistro, opened in 1963, and the Bistro Garden, both owned by former Romanoff's maitre d' Kurt Niklas, and Ma Maison, opened by Patrick Terrail (nephew of Claude Terrail, owner of the Paris' legendary Tour d'Argent), contributed to the city's new lust for bistro fare. Nonetheless, Chasen's was on solid ground for those who wanted to dress up and start their meal sipping a smart cocktail in comfortable surroundings peopled by members of L.A.'s social establishment and Holly-wood royalty.

Though Maude stayed out of the kitchen, she was particular about the way certain dishes were served. Instead of bread or rolls, a Chasen's meal always started off with a basket of Cheese Toast, and filling an evening's many Cheese Toast orders was a full-time job for one member of the kitchen staff. On busy nights, two people were needed just to keep the toast coming. "Maude would get very upset if it wasn't crisp," Boxer recalled. "It had to be crisp, hot and fresh. She was meticulous about it."

Dave died one month short of his seventy-fifth birthday, on June 16, 1973. At his funeral, Rabbi Edgar F. Magnin and Msgr. Paul Redmond presided. Jimmy Stewart read the eulogy, which was penned by Nunnally Johnson. Mervyn LeRoy, George Burns and George Jessel also spoke. The list of honorary pallbearers —

Maude's Salad

3 cups iceberg lettuce, chopped
3 cups romaine lettuce, chopped
½ cup chicory, chopped
2 cups fresh tomato, diced

Roquefort Dressing (see recipe below)
2 hard-cooked eggs, finely chopped
2 tablespoons fresh chives, finely chopped

In a medium bowl, toss the lettuces and tomato with some of the Roquefort Dressing. Spoon onto four plates. Sprinkle each serving with some of the chopped eggs and chives.

Serves four.

Roquefort Dressing

¼ cup Roquefort cheese
½ cup mayonnaise
⅓ cup dairy sour cream
1 tablespoon chili sauce

1 clove garlic, finely minced
1 teaspoon red wine vinegar
¼ teaspoon salt
⅛ teaspoon white pepper

Mash cheese slightly with a fork in a medium-size bowl. Stir in mayonnaise, sour cream, chili sauce, garlic, vinegar, salt and pepper. Blend well. Set aside and chill until needed.

from Jack Benny and William Holden to Robert Wagner — would have lit twenty marquees.

"What do you think the odds would be that a baby born of poor parents in Odessa in Southwest Russia in 1898 would one day wind up in Beverly Hills, California, rich, famous and loved by some of the most celebrated people on earth?" Stewart began. Dave's restaurant, Stewart also said, may have begun as "a branch office of Broadway," but it developed into "an aristocrat among restaurants. . . on every honors list of deluxe

kitchens. . ."

With Maude carrying the torch and the restaurant's loyal staff in place, Chasen's remained an aristocrat. "Chasen's has a reputation to maintain," Maude said. "It does change, although most of the changes go unnoticed. When I replace anything in the restaurant, it is always with exactly the same thing or as close to it as I can get. I am a stickler for detail and for excellence."

Chasen's regulars were growing older. Alfred Hitchcock's and Jimmy Durante's seventy-fifth birthday parties at the restaurant were both star-studded. The Jimmy Stewarts hosted their thirtieth wedding anniversary party there, and the Lew Wassermans threw an immense, Chasen's-catered fortieth anniversary bash on the Universal Studios lot. The restaurant continued to draw royalty, superstars and titans of business. In 1972 a *Los Angeles Times* writer described a "typical Sunday" at Chasen's: The tables were filled with notables ranging from Lucille Ball, Bing Crosby, Frank Sinatra and Nelson Riddle to former California Governor Edmund G. "Pat" Brown, Mitzi Gaynor and Dean Martin. "We have four generations of Kecks [Superior Oil] coming here. That's what I call staying power," Maude told *W* in 1980.

Chasen's staff remained expert at coddling stars. They knew that Bobby Darin wanted his chili served with rice and cheese. Richard Burton, who came in often with Elizabeth Taylor, favored buttered pumpernickel bread, French fries and a potato sandwich. And George Burns would order nothing but a couple of martinis and his favorite dessert, the coconut-encrusted Coupe Snowball .

Young Hollywood, although often diverted by hot spots like The Daisy and The Factory, also stopped in. Sally Field, Marlo Thomas and Bill Cosby were among those who turned out for the party Candy Spelling gave in honor of the airing of her producer-husband Aaron's five-hundredth television episode — from *The Mod Squad*.

Chasen's always guaranteed a good night of star watching. On one night, while Johnny Carson celebrated nineteen years with *The Tonight Show*

Lew Wasserman, center, escorted Ethel and Robert F. Kennedy to dinner.

Kay's Salad

2 cups fresh green beans, halved
  crosswise
2 cups romaine lettuce, shredded
1 cup onion, thinly sliced
1 large fresh tomato, diced

½ cup French Dressing (see recipe,
  page 42)
1 hard-cooked egg, finely chopped
2 tablespoons chives, finely minced

Cook the green beans in salted boiling water until nearly tender (*al dente*). Drain. Rinse several times in cold water and drain again.

Toss together beans, romaine, onions and tomatoes. Add dressing and toss again to coat well. Spoon salad onto four serving plates. Garnish each serving with chopped egg and a sprinkling of chives.

Serves four.

Cheese Toast

1 loaf sourdough French bread, cut into
  ¼-inch-thick slices

1 cup melted butter
2 cups freshly grated Parmesan
  cheese

Arrange bread slices on a broiler pan. Toast one side of bread until golden. Remove from broiler. Dip untoasted side of bread in butter, then coat buttered side heavily in Parmesan cheese. Place bread, cheese side up, under broiler. Broil until lightly browned. Serve piping hot.

Makes about 70 slices.

*Chasen's Ron Clint, left, and Tommy Gallagher
flanked Alfred Hitchcock at the director's seventy-
fifth birthday party.*

in one banquet room, Elizabeth
Taylor, her husband, Senator John
Warner, Rock Hudson and other
friends were marking her opening
night in *Little Foxes* in another.

When he wasn't on the road,
Frank Sinatra could be found once a
week at Chasen's, in the long booth
for ten in the front room, as well as
presiding over the many parties he
gave — from family birthdays to sup-
per parties for busloads of his friends
following his opening nights at local
theaters.

In the '50s, when he first started
frequenting Chasen's, Sinatra, true to
his tough-guy image, got into a brawl.
He was standing at the bar when he
heard someone make an anti-Semitic
remark. Sinatra punched the man, and
suddenly a group of the offender's
friends jumped on the entertainer.
The fight expanded when John
Wayne, who was dining in the restaurant and witnessed the attack, hurried
to Sinatra's rescue.

Mostly, though, Sinatra's evenings at Chasen's were tranquil. He
considered Chasen's a "safe restaurant" — if *paparazzi* waited outside,
he'd be ushered out a back door. Tommy Gallagher and the staff always enjoyed meeting his "tough taskmaster"
demands, remembers the crooner's
wife Barbara. That included his preference for half portions of everything,

Archive Photos/Fotos International

Sally Field and Steve Craig arrived for the Spelling party.

his dislike of garlic and his requests for the finest wines for his guests.

Sinatra had a particular fondness for the house Guacamole — which he liked spicy — and Chicken Curry. And, recalls Barbara Sinatra fondly, Christmases at the Sinatra home often included large Chasen's-catered buffets of turkey, ham and dressing as well as Chicken Curry, plus a little pasta "because this is an Italian home."

The Sinatras celebrated nine of eighteen anniversaries in the private Garden Room, always finishing off their meals with the Banana Cake, Frank's favorite dessert and one so delicious that the *Los Angeles Times* restaurant critic Lois Dwan said that it achieved "immortality" along with the famed chili.

In the late '70s food tastes began

to change radically in Los Angeles and celebrity chefs came on the scene. But Maude refused to change the food that made Chasen's successful. The restaurant continued to serve American dishes like Braised Yankee Pot Roast, Chicken Burger Forestierre with Mushroom Sauce, Cottage Fried Potatoes, Caesar Salad and Chopped Salad. And Continental cuisine, also a stronghold since the '40s, was apparent in dishes such as Roast Long Island Duckling Bigarade, Tournedos of Veal Orloff, Veal Chop Bon Mamma (later known as Veal Chop on Cocotte), Belgian Endive Salad with Red Beets and Walnuts — and two souffles: Carrot Souffle as a side dish and Grand Marnier Chocolate Souffle for dessert. Despite its meat-and-potatoes reputation, fish dishes were popular as well, including three salmon dishes — Baked Salmon with Pike Mousse, Salmon en Papillote and Salmon

Archive Photos/Fotos International

"Mod Squad" stars Michael Cole, left, and Peggy Lipton with Lou Adler at Spelling bash.

Braised Yankee Pot Roast

½ cup carrots, diced
¼ cup onion, diced
¼ cup celery, diced
1 tablespoon parsley, minced
4 cloves garlic, crushed and minced
1 teaspoon pepper
½ teaspoon salt
3 pounds triangle-tip beef roast
2 cups dry red wine such as
  Cabernet Sauvignon

½ cup all-purpose flour
salt and pepper to taste
2 to 3 tablespoons olive oil
2 tablespoons butter
1 cup tomato, diced
4 cups beef broth
½ cup tomato sauce
1 tablespoon cornstarch
water as needed

In a bowl, stir together the chopped carrots, onions, celery, parsley, garlic, pepper and salt.

Place the triangle-tip roast in a large nonmetal baking dish. Cover with vegetable mixture. Pour red wine over meat. Turn beef twice to coat thoroughly with the marinade. Cover and refrigerate overnight, turning meat several times.

Remove roast from marinade and reserve marinade. Pat meat dry. Sprinkle beef with salt and pepper and coat with flour. Shake off excess flour. Heat the olive oil in a skillet. Brown meat on both sides over medium-high heat. Remove from heat and set aside.

Preheat oven to 350 degrees. Drain marinade from the vegetables, reserving the juices. In the same skillet, melt butter. Saute the marinated vegetables for two minutes. Stir in the reserved juices, the diced tomato, three cups of the beef broth and tomato sauce. Bring mixture to boil.

Place beef in a roasting pan; pour hot vegetable mixture over it. Cover and roast for 3 to 3½ hours, or until meat is fork-tender, checking pan juices every 30 minutes. (Add water to pan juices as needed so that meat does not cook dry.) Transfer meat to a warm platter, cover and keep warm.

For the sauce: Skim the excess fat from pan juices. Transfer pan juices to a medium saucepan. Add the remaining cup of broth and 1 cup water mixed with the cornstarch. Cook and stir over medium-high heat until mixture thickens and boils. Reduce heat and simmer two minutes more. Taste for seasoning. Strain out vegetables.

Slice roast against the grain in thin slices. Serve with the sauce and potato pancakes, sauteed mushrooms and steamed carrots, peas and pearl onions.

Serves six.

Archive Photos/Fotos International

"That Girl" Marlo Thomas celebrated "The Mod Squad" at Chasen's.

Ravioli with Basil Sauce.

"Maude never said, 'Let's go *nouvelle*,'" Jeanne Voltz remembers. "She had this feeling that Chasen's was unique as it is — a good sturdy restaurant with a longtime reputation — and there was no reason to change it to something else."

Even the young turks on the restaurant scene understood. "It was one of *the* best places, one of the bright spots on the scene," says Michael McCarty, the brilliant young culinary upstart who opened Michael's in 1979. "It was a restaurant run by an individ-

ual who came up with a concept, ran the kitchen and created an aura that attracted clients who made it their club. It was long-lasting, real — and you knew it would be there. I grew up in New York where you respected these places as institutions."

"I always loved Chasen's," said Peter Morton, whose own restaurant, Morton's, also opened in 1979, and became a magnet for Hollywood stars and power brokers. "It had such a sense of history. Not many restaurants could achieve what they did with its persona, its ethos and its longevity."

Chicken Burger Forestierre

½ cup onion, minced
1 tablespoon butter
1½ pounds boneless, skinless
  chicken breasts*
1 egg yolk
1 cup fine dry bread crumbs
1 teaspoon pepper
¼ teaspoon salt
¼ teaspoon crushed dried thyme

1 tablespoon milk
1 teaspoon Worcestershire sauce
¼ teaspoon Tabasco sauce
¼ cup all-purpose flour
1 beaten egg
1 tablespoon water
1 tablespoon butter
1 tablespoon olive oil
Mushroom Sauce (see recipe on
  opposite page)

In a skillet saute onion in butter until tender but not brown. Remove from heat. Cut chicken into 1-inch pieces. Using a food processor, process chicken until coarsely ground, pulsing on and off several times. Turn chicken into a medium mixing bowl. Combine well with egg yolk, ½ cup bread crumbs, pepper, salt, thyme, milk, Worcestershire and Tabasco and the cooked onions.

In three shallow bowls place the remaining ½ cup bread crumbs, the ¼ cup flour and the egg beaten with water. Using a lightly floured surface, shape chicken mixture into four patties about ¾-inch thick. Coat each patty with bread crumbs, then coat with flour, then coat with egg mixture. Then coat again with bread crumbs. Place on waxed paper. (Patties can be covered and chilled several hours before serving time.)

To cook, preheat oven to 450 degrees. Heat 1 tablespoon butter and olive oil in a large oven-proof skillet. On the stove, brown patties over medium-high heat on both sides. Place pan in oven and bake patties five more minutes, or until no longer pink in center.

Serve burgers with mushroom sauce, steamed green beans and mashed potatoes if desired.

Serves four.

*Variation: For Veal Burger Forestierre, substitute 1½ pounds ground veal for the chicken.

Mushroom Sauce

2 cups mushrooms, sliced
1 shallot, finely chopped
2 tablespoons butter

¼ cup Marsala or sweet red wine
¼ teaspoon salt
1 cup Brown Sauce (see recipe below)

In a skillet, saute mushrooms and shallot in butter until tender. Add wine, bring to a boil. Reduce heat and simmer until wine is nearly evaporated. Stir in Brown Sauce. Season with salt to taste.

Brown Sauce

1 tablespoon butter
2 tablespoons onion, chopped
2 tablespoons carrots, chopped
2 tablespoons celery, chopped
1 tablespoon all-purpose flour
¼ cup dry red wine

2 cups beef broth
3 tablespoons tomato paste
1 teaspoon Worcestershire sauce
¼ teaspoon Tabasco
¼ teaspoon salt
¼ teaspoon pepper

Melt the butter in a medium saucepan. Saute the onions, carrots and celery over medium heat until well browned. Stir in flour and cook until it browns. Gradually stir in the red wine, broth and tomato paste. Stir constantly until mixture comes to a full boil. Reduce heat. Stir in Worcestershire, Tabasco, salt and pepper. Strain out vegetables.

Makes about 2¼ cups sauce. Can be frozen.

Cottage Fried Potatoes

2 large russet potatoes
2 tablespoons butter

2 tablespoons vegetable oil
salt and pepper to taste

Scrub potatoes and place in a pan with water to cover. Bring to boil. Reduce heat and simmer, partially covered, about 30 minutes or until tender. Cool and peel.

Slice the potatoes very thin, about ⅛-inch thick. Heat butter and oil in a 10-inch skillet. Arrange potato slices in several layers to cover bottom of pan. Saute potatoes, without turning, over medium-high heat until very brown on the bottom. Place a second oiled 10-inch skillet over the top of the potatoes. Hold the two pans together and very carefully invert the potatoes into second skillet. Cook till potatoes are very brown on the bottom. Turn the potatoes out in one layer onto paper towels to drain. Transfer to a serving plate. Cut in four wedges.

Serves four.

Caesar Salad

juice of 1½ lemons
2 tablespoons garlic oil*
1½ teaspoons Worcestershire sauce
6 tablespoons French Dressing
  (see recipe, page 42)
1 one-minute coddled egg (optional)

6 cups mixed salad greens
1 cup ½-inch croutons, preferably
  made from sourdough bread
1 teaspoon freshly ground pepper
4 tablespoons grated Parmesan cheese

*To make garlic oil, immerse one sliced garlic clove in oil. Let stand several hours. Remove garlic piece.

In a small bowl beat together lemon juice, garlic oil, Worcestershire sauce, French Dressing and coddled egg.

In a large wooden bowl, toss together salad greens, croutons, dressing mixture, pepper and, cheese. Serve immediately.

Serves four.

Chopped Salad

1½ cups iceberg lettuce, chopped
1½ cups romaine, chopped
1½ cups radicchio, chopped
⅓ cup hearts of palm, drained and
   cut into ½-inch pieces
⅓ cup cucumber, peeled and diced

⅓ cup canned artichoke hearts,
   drained and halved
½ cup garbanzo beans, drained
1 medium tomato, cut into 8 wedges
1 hard-cooked egg, finely chopped
2 tablespoons fresh chives, minced
French Dressing (see recipe, page 42)

Toss together lettuces, hearts of palm, cucumber, artichokes and garbanzo beans in a large bowl. Add tomatoes and some dressing, tossing to combine. Spoon salad onto four serving plates. Garnish each serving with chopped hard-cooked egg and a sprinkle of chives.

Serves four.

Gallagher Family collection

Frank and Barbara Sinatra, who spent many evenings at Chasen's, with captain Tommy Gallagher.

Roast Long Island Duckling Bigarade

2 5-pound Long Island ducklings
salt and pepper to taste
1 orange
½ cup dry red wine
1 tablespoon cornstarch

2 tablespoons orange juice
2 tablespoons currant jelly
1½ cups Brown Sauce (see recipe,
  page 57)
1 tablespoon brown sugar

Preheat oven to 450 degrees. Wash and pat ducklings dry. Remove necks, gizzards and hearts and rinse and pat dry. Reinsert necks, gizzards and hearts into duck cavities. Season with salt and pepper to taste. Place ducks on a rack in a large roasting pan. Roast, uncovered, for 15 minutes.

About ten minutes before the duck is done, use an orange zester to make long julienne strips from orange peel and set aside. Remove white pith from orange and place pith in a medium saucepan with half of the julienned orange zest. Chop orange pulp, reserving half. Place the remaining pulp in the saucepan with wine, cornstarch and orange juice.

Reduce heat to 375 degrees. Roast duck another 1 to 1¼ hours until a meat thermometer registers about 180 degrees.

Remove ducks from oven and transfer to a carving board. Cover with foil and let stand five minutes before carving. Strain juices, skimming off excess fat. Add remaining juices to the saucepan. Bring mixture to a boil. Reduce heat. Simmer two minutes. Stir in currant jelly, Brown Sauce and brown sugar until melted. Strain sauce and return to pan. Stir in the reserved pulp. Carve duck. Serve with sauce and reserved julienned orange peel.

Serves four.

Tournedoes of Veal Orloff

Perigoudine Sauce (see recipe below)
12 thin (¼-inch) slices veal
all-purpose flour as needed
salt and pepper to taste
2 tablespoons butter
¼ cup celery, minced
¼ cup onion, minced

¼ cup carrot, minced
¼ cup mushrooms, minced
¼ teaspoon crushed dried thyme
⅓ cup all-purpose flour
2 tablespoons butter
2 tablespoons olive oil

Prepare Perigoudine Sauce, keep warm over low heat while preparing veal. (Or cover and chill mixture to reheat at serving time.)

Preheat oven to 400 degrees. Place veal slices on a sheet of waxed paper dusted with flour. Season on both sides with salt and pepper. Melt butter in a skillet. Saute celery, onions, carrots and mushrooms until very tender. Stir in thyme, salt and pepper to taste. Spoon 2 teaspoons of vegetable mixture onto half of each veal slice. Fold other half of veal over filling. Secure edge with a wooden pick. Coat filled veal slice with flour.

In a large oven-proof skillet heat butter and oil. Saute veal on all sides over medium-high heat until well-browned. For well-done meat, place skillet, covered, in oven for five to seven minutes. Serve two tournedoes on each plate with Perigoudine Sauce.

Serves six.

Perigoudine Sauce

1 tablespoon butter
¼ cup mushrooms, chopped
1 shallot, minced

¼ cup dry red wine
1½ cups Brown Sauce (see recipe, page 57)

Melt butter in a medium saucepan. Saute mushrooms and shallot until well done. Stir in wine, bring to boil. Reduce heat and simmer till mixture is reduced by half. Stir in Brown Sauce. Season to taste.

Veal Chop Bon Mamma or en Cocotte

2 pounds veal loin chops (6 chops)
⅓ cup all-purpose flour
salt and pepper to taste
2 tablespoons butter
2 tablespoons olive oil
2 cups mushrooms, quartered

2 cups baby potatoes, quartered and cooked
½ cup pearl onions, cooked
1 shallot, minced
2 cups Brown Sauce (see recipe, page 57)
½ cup dry white wine
1 tablespoon chives, minced

Preheat oven to 400 degrees. Coat veal chops on all sides with flour. Season to taste with salt and pepper. In a large oven-proof skillet heat 1 tablespoon each of the butter and oil. Saute chops on both sides over medium heat until well-browned. Place skillet in oven. Cover and bake chops for five to ten minutes more, or to desired doneness.

Meanwhile, in another skillet heat remaining butter and oil. Saute mushrooms, baby potatoes, onions and shallot until golden brown. Stir in Brown Sauce and wine. Bring to boil. Reduce heat and simmer two minutes more. To serve, pour sauce over each chop. Sprinkle with chives.

Serves six.

Belgian Endive Salad with Red Beets and Walnuts

4 heads Belgian endive
1 8-ounce can beets, chilled

½ cup broken walnuts
French Dressing (see recipe, page 42)

Trim ½ inch off the bottom of each head of endive. Cut endive crosswise into ½-inch slices. Place endive in a medium salad bowl. Drain beets, rinse and drain well. Add to salad with walnuts. Toss with French Dressing. Serve at once.

Serves four.

Carrot Souffle

1 pound carrots, peeled and sliced
3 eggs
3 tablespoons granulated sugar
3 tablespoons all-purpose flour
½ teaspoon vanilla

¼ teaspoon ground nutmeg
½ cup (1 stick) melted butter
¼ cup finely chopped walnuts or
  crushed corn flakes
1 tablespoon brown sugar
1 tablespoon melted butter

Cook carrots in boiling salted water until very tender; drain. Butter a 1½-quart souffle dish or straight-sided casserole dish. Preheat oven to 350 degrees.

Place carrots in food processor or blender with eggs, sugar, flour, vanilla and nutmeg. Process until pureed. Add butter and process again. Turn mixture into buttered souffle dish. Bake for 35 to 40 minutes or until souffle is slightly puffed and golden. Sprinkle chopped walnuts and brown sugar over top of souffle. Drizzle with the melted butter. Return to oven for 10 to 15 minutes or till the top is crisp and golden.

Serves four to six.

Grand Marnier Chocolate Souffle

butter as needed	2 tablespoons all-purpose flour
granulated sugar as needed	2 tablespoons sugar
2 tablespoons Grand Marnier liqueur	4 eggs, separated
2 tablespoons butter	1 tablespoon vanilla
2 ounces (2 squares) semisweet	¼ teaspoon cream of tartar
chocolate, broken up	½ cup granulated sugar
1 cup milk	Grand Marnier Sauce
	(see recipe below)

Butter four 10-ounce custard cups or individual souffle dishes. Sprinkle sugar inside dishes. Then place 1½ teaspoons Grand Marnier into the bottom of each prepared souffle dish. Place dishes on a baking sheet.

In a medium-size heavy saucepan melt butter and chocolate together, being careful not to burn it. Stir together the milk, flour and sugar in a separate bowl until dissolved. Whisk into chocolate mixture and bring to a boil. Reduce heat and simmer two minutes. Remove from heat and cool five minutes.

Stir in egg yolks, beating rapidly with a wire whisk. Place saucepan in refrigerator for five minutes to cool. Preheat oven to 400 degrees.

In a large mixing bowl, beat egg whites with vanilla and cream of tartar on high speed of electric mixer until foamy. Gradually add the ½ cup sugar, 2 tablespoons at a time, beating well after each addition, until mixture forms stiff peaks (tips stand straight when beaters are lifted).

With a rubber spatula, fold chocolate mixture in an up-and-over motion gently into egg whites, until no streaks of white appear in mixture (do not stir). Turn mixture into prepared souffle dishes. Bake for 20 minutes or until puffy and brown. Meanwhile, prepare Grand Marnier sauce.

Remove souffles from oven when done. Serve immediately with Grand Marnier sauce.

Serves four.

Grand Marnier Sauce

1 cup milk	1 to 2 tablespoons Grand Marnier liqueur
1 tablespoon cornstarch	2 to 3 tablespoons sugar

In a medium heavy saucepan combine milk and cornstarch. Bring mixture to boil, stirring constantly. Reduce heat and simmer one minute. Remove from heat. Stir in Grand Marnier, then sweeten to taste with sugar.

Baked Salmon with Pike Mousse

Pike Mousse (see recipe below)
1½ pounds whole salmon fillet
salt and pepper to taste
1 tablespoon butter
3 medium shallots, finely chopped
½ cup chicken broth

½ cup dry white wine
1 cup heavy whipping cream
6 tablespoons butter, cut up
1 teaspoon lemon juice
garnish: steamed potatoes

Prepare Pike Mousse; cover mixture and refrigerate while preparing salmon.

Preheat oven to 400 degrees. Cut salmon fillet crosswise into six fillets. Season on both sides with salt and pepper. Butter a 12x18-inch baking dish and sprinkle the chopped shallots in bottom of dish. Arrange the salmon fillets over shallots. Spoon a heaping teaspoonful of pike mousse over each salmon fillet. If necessary, rinse spoon each time for ease in handling mousse.

Pour chicken broth and wine carefully into bottom of dish, not touching the mousse. Bake 15 to 20 minutes, or until the mousse is light golden brown and puffed, and salmon flakes easily.

Carefully transfer salmon fillets to six serving plates. Keep warm. Strain cooking liquid, if necessary, into a small saucepan. Bring liquid to boil. Simmer until reduced by half. Add the 1 cup heavy cream, whisking constantly. Add butter piece by piece, stirring constantly until butter is melted. Stir in lemon juice. Taste for seasoning. Pour sauce around each salmon fillet. Garnish each serving with steamed potatoes.

Serves six.

Pike Mousse

8 ounces pike or other white fish fillets
1 whole egg
1 egg, separated
¼ teaspoon salt

⅛ teaspoon pepper
⅛ teaspoon ground nutmeg
⅓ cup heavy whipping cream

Cut pike into ½-inch chunks. Place in food processor, processing in short bursts until ground. Add the whole egg and one egg yolk, salt, pepper and nutmeg. Process for a few seconds. With the machine running, pour ⅓ cup whipping cream through the hole in lid and process until mixture is well blended. In a medium bowl beat the egg white on high speed of electric mixer until stiff peaks form. Fold pike mixture into egg white until no traces of egg white remain. Refrigerate until used.

Guacamole

2 large ripe avocados	¼ cup onion, chopped
2 tablespoons fresh lemon juice	6 to 8 serrano chilies,* seeded and minced
¼ cup fresh tomato, diced	1 teaspoon salt

Peel avocados and remove pits. In medium bowl, mash avocado pulp and lemon juice together with a fork. Stir in tomato, onion, chili peppers and salt. Serve immediately or cover the surface of the guacamole with plastic wrap and chill up to several hours before serving.

Makes 2½ cups dip.

*Wear gloves to work with the chilies and wash your hands thoroughly in warm soapy water after handling.

Salmon en Papillote

2 tablespoons butter
½ cup onions, cut in 1½-inch julienne
½ cup carrots, cut in 1½-inch julienne
½ cup mushrooms, julienned
¼ cup celery, cut in 1½-inch julienne
2 tablespoons fresh tarragon, minced
salt and pepper to taste
1½ pounds whole salmon fillet
parchment paper

2 tablespoons olive oil
2 tablespoons shallots, minced
fresh tarragon leaves
¼ cup chicken broth
¼ cup white wine
4 tablespoons butter
1 cup Beurre Blanc Sauce
  (see recipe on opposite page)

In large skillet, melt butter. Saute onions, carrots, mushrooms and celery for five minutes or until vegetables are nearly tender (*al dente*). Season with tarragon, salt and pepper to taste. Cover pan. Remove from heat and let stand while preparing salmon.

Preheat oven to 450 degrees. Remove any skin from salmon fillet. Cut crosswise in half. Cut each half into six fillets about ½-inch thick each. Season fillets on both sides with salt and pepper. Cut four 14-inch wide pieces of parchment paper. Fold one piece in half. Cut a heart shape from the folded side so the paper opens up to display a full heart shape. Repeat with remaining three pieces of parchment. Brush one side of each heart with olive oil.

For each serving lay a parchment heart oil-side down on a large baking sheet with sides. Spoon one-fourth of the vegetables on one side of the heart, leaving a 2-inch border around the edge. Lay three salmon fillets over vegetables. Sprinkle salmon with one-fourth of the chopped shallots and some fresh tarragon leaves. Sprinkle with 1 tablespoon of the broth and 1 tablespoon of the wine. Dot salmon with butter.

Fold other half of heart over salmon and vegetables. Starting at the top of the heart, fold under the two edges of paper several times, continuing around the heart to the bottom. Make sure to fold securely several times. When you reach the bottom of the heart, fold the point under to hold paper in place. Repeat to make four paper packets. Arrange packets on the flat baking sheet.

Bake for about eight to ten minutes or until the paper is puffed and beginning to brown around the edges. Serve immediately by carefully cutting each packet open on the serving plate. Serve with Beurre Blanc Sauce.

Serves four.

Beurre Blanc Sauce

4 shallots, minced
1 cup white wine
1 cup chicken stock

1 cup sweet butter
2 drops Tabasco sauce
dash soy sauce

Combine shallots and wine in saucepan over medium heat until wine has evaporated. Add stock and bring to a boil. Lower heat and thicken with butter, adding a tablespoon at a time and stirring constantly. Add Tabasco and soy sauces. Strain through a fine mesh strainer. Mix in blender for 15 seconds.

Makes 1½ cups.

Salmon Ravioli with Basil Sauce

Basil Sauce (see recipe below)
Buerre Blanc Sauce (see recipe, page 69)
1 7½ -ounce can chunk-style salmon
salt and pepper to taste

96 wonton skins
1 beaten egg white
1 teaspoon water
for garnish: fresh diced tomatoes
and basil leaves

Prepare Basil Sauce. Just before cooking ravioli, prepare Beurre Blanc sauce. Cover and keep warm over low heat.

Drain salmon, removing all bones and skin. Chop coarsely. Place in a bowl and stir in 2 tablespoons of the Basil Sauce, salt and pepper to taste. For round ravioli, use a 3-inch circular cutter to cut circles from wonton skins. Discard scraps. For traditional square ravioli, leave pieces square. In a small bowl whisk the egg white and water. Brush the edges of two wonton skins with egg white mixture. Spoon 1 teaspoon salmon mixture onto center of one wonton. Place second wonton over it, egg white side down, and press firmly around all edges to seal. Place filled ravioli on a baking sheet. Cover with plastic wrap to keep them from drying out. Repeat with remaining wonton skins and filling to make 48 ravioli. (If preparing ahead, cover ravioli with another layer of plastic wrap and refrigerate. Can be made up to several hours before serving time.)

To cook ravioli, bring a large pan of water to boiling. Reduce heat to simmer. Add ravioli, half at a time, to pot. Simmer three to five minutes or until nearly tender (*al dente*). With a slotted spoon, transfer ravioli to colander to drain. (Do not rinse.) Keep warm while cooking remaining ravioli.

For each serving, arrange eight ravioli on a serving plate. Serve topped with Beurre Blanc Sauce and garnish with remaining Basil Sauce. Sprinkle with diced tomatoes and garnish with a basil leaf.

Serves six.

Basil Sauce

¼ cup fresh basil, minced
2 tablespoons fresh tarragon, minced
2 tablespoons fresh chives, minced
2 shallots, minced

2 cloves garlic, crushed, then minced
½ cup olive oil
½ teaspoon salt
½ teaspoon pepper

In a small bowl stir together basil, tarragon, chives, shallots, garlic, oil, salt and pepper until well combined. Cover and refrigerate until needed. (Sauce can be made up to several days ahead.)

Makes about ¾ cup.

In 1991, the five living U. S. presidents, from left, George Bush, Ronald Reagan, Jimmy Carter, Gerald Ford and Richard Nixon gathered for the dedication of the Reagan Library.

CHAPTER SIX

The President's Beef

Chasen's was part of our courtship, our romance, our life.
— **Nancy Reagan, 1995**

The relationship between Ronald and Nancy Reagan and Chasen's was formally cemented one night in February 1952 when the couple, dining in their favorite booth — third to the left as you entered the front room — made plans and set the date for their wedding. Ever after, they considered it their second home, and their many dinners there throughout the '80s and '90s distinguished it as Reagan country. But Chasen's appeal was nonpartisan. Every American president since 1945 ate a Chasen's meal. And even though Franklin D. Roosevelt didn't dine there, Eleanor did.

Chasen's supplied a sit-down dinner for about 5,000 for Dwight D. Eisenhower at the old Pan Pacific Auditorium. Beverly Hills Savings and Loan magnate Bart Lytton hired Chasen's to cater a fundraising dinner at his home for

President Harry Truman, center, shared an evening with George Jessel and California governor Edmund G. "Pat" Brown.

John F. Kennedy's presidential campaign, and Lew and Edie Wasserman did the same for Bill Clinton at their home when he was running for president. The restaurant was a frequent choice of Richard M. Nixon, who enjoyed Hobo Steak, whenever he was staying at the Western White House in San Clemente. Presidential adviser Henry A. Kissinger was a regular dinner companion of Nixon, and Kissinger came on his own as well. In 1972, Chasen's was the target of its one and only bomb threat about a half hour after Kissinger finished his dinner. Nixon was also a Chasen's regular as part of a male foursome that included his banker friend Bebe Rebozo after they headed off to Rams football games. Nixon even had a hot line to the White House installed in Dave's office.

Years later, when two caterers were brought in to handle the thou-

sands of guests at the grand opening of the Richard Nixon Presidential Library and Birthplace in Yorba Linda on July 19, 1990, Chasen's was hired to provide lunch solely for ex-Presidents Nixon, Gerald Ford and Reagan and for President George Bush and their wives, as well as Nixon daughters Julie and Tricia and their respective husbands, David Eisenhower and Ed Cox.

"We thought, 'Who is caterer to the presidents in Los Angeles?'" explained the Library's Sandy Quinn. "And it was Chasen's."

Throughout their lives, however, it was Ronald Reagan and his wife, Nancy, who were instantly identified with Chasen's. In fact, Reagan was a frequent customer back when it was the Southern Pit.

It was the restaurant where Nancy Davis and Ronald Reagan dined most often during their two and a half years of dating. "We both loved the feel of Chasen's. We liked Maude and Dave, and at that time we'd always see friends there. It was just comfortable," said Mrs. Reagan.

Their late-afternoon nuptials at the Little Brown Church in the San Fernando Valley on March 4, 1952, were strictly private, arranged in secret because of the intense press speculation about when and where and if the event would happen. Unbeknownst to the Reagans, however, captain Tommy Gallagher overheard them making marriage plans the month before at Chasen's and waited outside the church to get the first glimpse of the newlyweds.

From then on, the Chasen-Reagan relationship was official. After the wedding, a picture of the Reagans with Maude went up over their booth. Dave personally escorted the bride to

his favorite downtown markets and taught her how to pick out the best cuts of meat. And, the former First Lady said, "With each child I had, Dave sent dinner to Cedars-Sinai hospital every night."

Although he enjoyed eating everything at Chasen's, Boiled Beef Belmont, the Tuesday special, was Ronald Reagan's particular passion. A Jewish dish with origins in Eastern Europe and related to the French pot-au-feu, the Chasen's version was served as two separate courses. It started off with a steaming bowl of beef vegetable soup infused with noodles and matzo balls and was followed by a plate of four slices of beef served with green tomato pickles and creamed horseradish.

Reagan never asked to have the dish made specially for him on other nights, Nancy Reagan said. However,

Clark and Kay Gable joined President Dwight D. Eisenhower.

Boiled Beef Belmont

3 pounds short ribs of beef	1½ cups carrots, sliced diagonally
2 cups beef broth	1 cup leeks, sliced diagonally
2 bay leaves	1 cup celery, sliced diagonally
2 sprigs parsley	½ cup lima beans
1 teaspoon dried thyme	4 ounces long egg noodles
2 teaspoons salt	salt and pepper to taste
1½ teaspoons pepper	Matzo Balls (see recipe below)

Place short ribs and broth in a large Dutch oven. Add water to cover ribs. Bring mixture to a boil. Reduce heat and simmer. Skim foam from broth. Make a bouquet garni by tying bay leaves, parsley sprigs and thyme into a cheesecloth bundle with kitchen string. Place bundle in the broth with salt and pepper. Simmer, covered, for about 1½ hours or until meat is very tender and falls off the bone.

Remove bouquet garni and strain the broth. Return broth and meat to pan. Stir in carrots, leeks and celery. Bring mixture to boil. Reduce heat and simmer, covered, for 10 minutes or until vegetables are tender. Return mixture to boil. Add lima beans and egg noodles, cooking just until noodles are nearly tender (*al dente*). Remove meat. Separate meat from bones. Have soup at room temperature or warmer and add Matzo Balls; simmer for 5 minutes. Serve first with 2 or 3 matzo balls per bowl. Slice meat and garnish plate with green tomato pickles and horseradish.

Serves six.

Matzo Balls

4 tablespoons melted fat or oil	1 to 2 tablespoons salt, if desired
4 large eggs, slightly beaten	4 tablespoons soup stock or water
1 cup Manischewitz matzo meal	

Blend fat or oil with eggs. Mix matzo meal with salt. Combine these two mixtures and blend well. Add soup stock or water and mix until uniform. Cover mixing bowl and place in refrigerator for 15 minutes.

In a 3-quart pot, bring 2 quarts of water to a full boil, adding a pinch of salt if desired. From the refrigerated mixture, form about 16 matzo balls, each 1 inch in diameter. Reduce flame and drop matzo balls into the gently boiling water. Cover pot and cook 30 to 40 minutes. Remove matzo balls from water and add to Boiled Beef Belmont recipe.

Mrs. Bart Lytton, second from right, hosted presidential nominee John F. Kennedy, California governor Edmund G. "Pat" Brown and his wife Bernice.

they often made sure to come on Tuesdays. And to make certain he got his beef, Mrs. Reagan generally called ahead to reserve two orders, one for him and one for her.

The rules were bent the night after Reagan was elected president. On that historic Wednesday, Ron Clint recalled, "The president-elect ordered Beef Belmont."

After Reagan became governor of California and then president of the United States, those cherished Tuesday night dinners became a rarity. Nevertheless, in the '80s, a special back door was installed for the few times a year when he was in town. On those occasions, the couple's close friends typically entertained the Reagans at Chasen's or at their homes with Chasen's catered meals. The group included Betty and William

Wilson, Reagan's envoy to the Vatican; Erlenne and Dr. Norman Sprague Jr.; original "Kitchen Cabinet" member Henry Salvatori and his wife, Grace; and Charles Wick, whom Reagan appointed director of the U.S. Information Agency, and his wife, Mary Jane. "You didn't even have to think about it — let's go to Chasen's," Wick said.

"If you wanted to take the Reagans to dinner, you'd ask, 'Do you want to go to Chasen's?' They'd always say yes," their good friend Armand Deutsch recalls of the many evenings he and his wife, Harriet, dined with the Reagans. Their small groups (which often included Betsy Bloomingdale, steel tycoon Earle Jorgensen and his wife, Marion, the Wilsons, Wicks and Spragues) would convene first for cocktails in Dave's office and

Maude greeted President Richard Nixon, a Chasen's regular.

tenure that anyone can recall Chasen's Chili being shipped to Washington, D.C.

After that, Mrs. Reagan's birthday barbecues were a summertime fixture at Rancho del Cielo, the Reagans' ranch north of Santa Barbara. Every year the Western-style parties for more than one hundred friends were hosted by the Wilsons and Jorgensens. Early in the morning three Chasen's catering trucks, loaded with chili, ribs and chicken for barbecuing and, naturally, birthday cake, would make the trek north to Santa Barbara and up the dirt road leading to the house, where they were always met with a thorough security check. "Those were the most wonderful birthdays," Mrs. Reagan recalls fondly.

On November 4, 1991, the Ronald Reagan Presidential Library in Simi Valley was dedicated. Four of the country's five living presidents — Ford, Bush, Carter and Reagan — were treated to a Chasen's meal. Richard Nixon was scheduled to attend the lunch, but when his wife, Pat, fell ill in the 108-degree weather, they made a quick getaway instead.

On the menu was fresh English sole, Chinese pea pods, new potatoes with basil and Coupe Snowball for dessert.

Coupe Snowball is a variation of Coupe Alexander, which joined the perennial list when Dave's good friend Bernard Schwab, one of the Schwab's

then sit down to dinner at a long, corner booth for ten in the front room.

As Chasen's became the local eatery for the Reagans' circle of friends, so too did they choose it for most of their entertaining. That was the case when movie producer Walter Mirisch and his wife, Pat, hosted a "Mr. Smith Goes to Washington" sendoff party for William French Smith and his wife, Jean, after he was appointed attorney general.

During Reagan's first year in office, Mrs. Reagan's Fourth of July birthday was celebrated on the grounds of the historic Woodlawn Plantation near Mt. Vernon. It was the only occasion during Reagan's

Pharmacy brothers, sold him his over-supply of anisette. "Dave started playing around with it," Tommy Gallagher said. Finally, he came up with the idea of pouring it over a scoop of vanilla ice cream blanketed with toasted coconut. An even more popular variation of the dessert, Coupe Snowball, was devised when chocolate syrup was substituted for the anisette.

Reagan was dining at Chasen's one night after his retirement when he was told that a group of patrons upstairs was overwhelmed to hear he was there. He decided to say hello and ambled into their private dining room. "Well, you've come to the best restaurant in America," he told them.

Reagan celebrated his eightieth birthday party at Chasen's. And the restaurant, though shuttered for nearly a year, reopened on February 6, 1996, to mark his eighty-fifth. Boiled Beef Belmont could not be served to such a large crowd, so the party dined on the Reagans' other favorites: Scottish smoked salmon, Chicken Pot Pie and Coupe Snowballs.

Coupe Snowball

1 pint vanilla ice cream   Hershey's chocolate syrup
2 tablespoons toasted shredded coconut

Scoop ice cream into four dishes. Sprinkle toasted coconut over ice cream. Serve immediately with chocolate syrup. Let guests spoon on their own syrup.

Makes four servings.

Coupe Alexander

Coupe Alexander is made exactly as Coupe Snowball, except that anisette is substituted for chocolate syrup. Before serving, drizzle 1 teaspoon of liqueur over each serving.

*President Jimmy Carter, shown here with Maude, was among the
many presidents who dined on Chasen's chow.*

*At the family retreat, Rancho del Cielo in Santa
Barbara, Nancy Reagan blows out her birthday
candles while the President and son Ron look on.*

Gallagher Family collection

President George Bush poses with Ron Clint, left, and Tommy Gallagher.

Mike Guastella photo

Celebrating his eightieth birthday at Chasen's, President Reagan cut the cake as the former First Lady beamed.

After the 1994 Academy Awards, Madonna and Quentin Tarantino, who won an Oscar for Best Original Screenplay for "Pulp Fiction," partied at Chasen's in March 1995.

CHAPTER SEVEN

The Last Act

The barbarians at the studio gates are closing down Chasen's, a restaurant that has meant to Hollywood what Maxim's has to Paris and "21" to New York.
— **The New Yorker, February 20, 1995**

When word got out in early 1995 that Chasen's doors would close in a few months, it was just like the old days — impossible to get a table. Until then, business had fallen. In recent years Maude's health had declined, the old guard was dying off, and young restaurant goers were attracted to new, trendy restaurants with adventurous cuisine and laid-back atmosphere, like Wolfgang Puck's Spago and Chinois.

Chasen's effort to attract new customers by opening for lunch the last four years wasn't enough to rev up business, nor, in the final year, were Monday singles nights, fashion shows or cabarets featuring contemporary composers.

But now, in its last days, the restaurant was booked solid, not only the choice booths in the front rooms but the banquet rooms as well. Elizabeth Taylor ordered dozens of quarts of Chasen's Chili for safekeeping. Jack Nicholson, Whoopi Goldberg, Clint Eastwood, Tom Cruise, Tom Hanks and Sharon Stone occupied tables where Humphrey Bogart, Cary Grant, Joan Crawford and Marilyn Monroe once held court. And on successive evenings, movie mogul Jeffrey Katzenberg gave a birthday party for Elton John, the Charles Wicks entertained Margaret Thatcher, and the Norman Spragues tossed a party celebrating the Earle Jorgensens' wedding anniversary.

"It's madness," Ron Clint said of the crush.

In March, Miramax Pictures took over the restaurant for an old-style, star-packed Academy Awards party. The *Pulp Fiction* crowd — including star John Travolta and director Quentin Tarantino, clutching his Oscar for Best Original Screenplay

(won with Roger Avary) — mingled with Best Actress winner Jessica Lange, Best Supporting Actress winner Dianne Wiest and nominee Jodie Foster, plus Madonna, Jay Leno, Holly Hunter and Hollywood's hot dating duo Uma Thurman and Timothy Hutton.

Maybe Chasen's had matured into the "sedate, clubby eating place of Hollywood's *ancien regime*," as *Los Angeles Times* society writer Bill Higgins wrote, but it was going out "in a flambe of glory." The *ancien regime*, L.A.'s party types discovered a few years too late, wasn't a bad regime at all.

As Barbara Davis, one of the town's most renowned hostesses put it, "If they had the last night two years earlier, it wouldn't have gone out of business."

But sentiments weren't enough to keep the place going. Chasen's was

"Pulp Fiction" star John Travolta, who was nominated for Best Actor, and his wife Kelly Preston worked the party in Chasen's wood-paneled dining room on Academy Awards night.

joining L.A.'s list of departed institutions, legends that would become only memories. The land that Dave bought up parcel by parcel was to be sold to a developer who planned to raze the sprawling, white colonial-style edifice with its familiar green awning and erect another shopping center.

On closing night film producer Richard Zanuck remembered weekly dinners with his father, Darryl F. Zanuck, who once was head of production at the 20th Century Fox studio. Nancy Reagan called to say goodbye to all the staff. The Wassermans took a large table. "This would never happen in Europe," record producer Quincy Jones complained. "It's so ridiculous. It just blows me away. I'll be glad when we learn how to respect our heritage and history."

"Maybe it wasn't noisy enough," director Arthur Hiller, president of the Academy of Motion Pictures Arts and Sciences, observed, trying to understand why it was going.

"Please," sighed actress Jennifer Jones Simon, "tell me it's an April Fools'."

But it wasn't a joke. On April 1, 1995, Chasen's closed its doors. An era was over.

Courtesy Miramax Films

Jody Foster and friend Randy Stone helped bid goodbye to Chasen's at the restaurant's final Oscar-night party.

ACKNOWLEDGMENTS

I learned in the process of writing this book that my grandfather liked sitting in Billy Grady Jr.'s booth whenever he dined at Chasen's, that my father was raised in Dave Chasen's hometown in Connecticut and that my great uncle presided at Dave's funeral. Those people gave me a very direct link to Chasen's past.

My own connection? Two of the true highlights of my career as a social editor and writer occurred while covering Chasen's-catered events — the extraordinary 20th Century Fox dinner for Queen Elizabeth II and the exquisite opening party for Neiman Marcus Beverly Hills. Never mind the evening in the 1980s when I wasn't permitted inside the restaurant to cover a party for President and Mrs. Reagan and had to report from the sidewalk.

The gentlemanly Ralph M. Woodworth, Chasen's chief operating officer, was my conduit to the restaurant. Without Ron Clint, who was the restaurant's manager for almost four decades, to lean on, this book would not have been feasible. And I am grateful to have secured an interview with Tommy Gallagher, who worked at Chasen's throughout its heyday and was a key member of Dave's catering department, shortly before he passed away; his family was always cooperative. Chasen's Orhan Arli, John Laione, Bernard Klerlein and Pepe Ruiz were also very important to the research.

Special thanks also to William Holmes in the *Los Angeles Times* library; Lisa Cavalier in Nancy Reagan's office; Lewis and Lynn Blumberg, Erlenne Sprague, Jean Smith, Charles and Mary Jane Wick, Arthur Marx, Bruce David Colen, Robert Lloyd, Arlene Campbell of The Blue Ribbon of the Music Center of Los Angeles County; Burkes Hamner, Joan Luther, Alan Berliner, Stacey Behlmer of the Academy of Motion Picture Arts and Sciences' Margaret Herrick Library; members of the charitable organization SHARE; Joyce MacRae, Patricia Fox, Beverly Morgan and Kirk Girou of Neiman Marcus Beverly Hills; Kelly Jones and Rob Lebow at 20th Century Fox; Mark Gill, Andrea Galvin, Janet Hill and

87

Karen Paul at Miramax Pictures; Lynda Schuler at the Ronald Reagan Presidential Foundation; Sandy Quinn of the Richard Nixon Presidential Library and Birthplace; and Thomas Kunkel for sharing his exceptional knowledge of Harold Ross. Shortly before her death, Audrey Meadows Six graciously shared her memories with me.

I also want to thank Maude Chasen's daughter Kay and her husband Tom McKay for allowing us to publish this book. They are hoping that their son Scott will someday be able to carry on the Chasen's tradition.

Cheers, again, to my elite team at Angel City Press — Jean Penn, Scott McAuley and Paddy Calistro. And to home economist consultant Marlene Brown for her work on the recipes.

Lastly, my ace legal team — dad Eugene Goodwin and husband Keith Klevan — who went beyond the call to make sure this project was a go.

—Betty Goodwin

Recipe Index

Index

ABOUT THE AUTHOR

Betty Goodwin

Betty Goodwin has written about the entertainment industry, style and the social scene in Los Angeles for many years. *Chasen's: Where Hollywood Dined, Recipes and Memories* follows her popular history of Los Angeles restaurants, *Hollywood du Jour: Lost Recipes of Legendary Hollywood Haunts.*

She is coauthor of *Marry Me! Courtships and Proposals of Legendary Couples* and *L.A. Inside Out: The Architecture and Interiors of America's Most Colorful City.*

The former society editor of the *Los Angeles Herald Examiner*, she now covers the social scene and fashion for the *Los Angeles Times* and contributes to many national magazines.

Born in Los Angeles, Goodwin often found herself ensconced in one of Chasen's red-leather booths observing the world's *glitterati* as they dined in Hollywood style.

Sheryl Winter

Graphic designer Sheryl Winter is an award-winning print designer and illustrator working in Los Angeles. A graduate of renowned Otis Parsons Art Institute of Design in Los Angeles and California State University at Northridge, she has spent nearly a decade as art director for cookbooks, children's books and general interest works. A native of Los Angeles, she dined at Chasen's many times.

Chasen's

Chasen's was produced on an Apple Macintosh IIci. Programs used include QuarkXPress, Adobe Illustrator and Adobe Photoshop. The font used in the body text is Goudy 12 point; the font used in the chapter heads is Linoscript 35 point. Chasen's was printed in Chelsea, Michigan.

IN PRAISE OF
Hollywood du Jour

BY BETTY GOODWIN

"Goodwin has a knack for
unearthing L.A.'s heritage."
—*Los Angeles Times*

"This one delivers
the dish
and the dishes."
—*Los Angeles Times Syndicate*

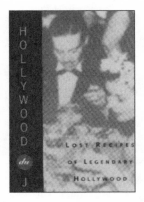

"A loving look at Tinsel-
town's culinary past."
—*San Francisco Examiner*

"A beautiful little book
... pithy essays and excel-
lent period illustrations."
—*L.A. Weekly*

"A terrific read and fascinating book."
—*Bon Appetit*

Hollywood du Jour is a charmingly designed hardcover gift book that *Bon Appetit* magazine called "a fascinating book full of recipes, photographs and lore." Author Betty Goodwin profiles Hollywood's eighteen best-remembered, but long-shut-tered restaurants and showcases their best-loved recipes.

Taking readers from the Cocoanut Grove and the Brown Derby to Ma Maison and Trumps, this nostalgic journey for the taste buds begins at a time when moviedom ate chopped salad in hot spots shaped like hats, nibbled rumaki in tropical huts and danced the night away in clubs more exotic than any movie set. Chronicling stories of Hollywood's past, Goodwin is a guide through seven mouth-watering decades of Hollywood's culinary history — the restaurants and food that nourished stars from the Golden Age to the recent past.

The list of more than thirty fondly recalled recipes includes Brown Derby's famed Cobb Salad and Grapefruit Cake, Tick Tock Tea Room's treasured Sticky Orange Rolls, Cyrano's Onion Soup, Cock 'n' Bull's Welshman's Rabbit and its legendary Moscow Mule cocktail, Scandia's authentic Scandinavian gravlaks, Romanoff's unparalleled Chocolate Souffle, Schwab's Pharmacy's famous chocolate soda, and many, many more. *Hollywood du Jour: Lost Recipes of Legendary Hollywood Haunts* is a must-have for any collector of hard-to-find recipes, plus it's an irresistible melange of Hollywood nostalgia.

Hollywood du Jour, ISBN 1-883318-22-X, $15.95; call 800-949-8039.

Angel City Press

Angel City Press, Incorporated, was established in 1992 and is dedicated to the publication of high-quality nonfiction and poetry. Angel City Press is located by the sea in Santa Monica, Calfornia.